BEETLE BATTLES

One Scientist's Journey of Adventure and Discovery

Doug Emlen

Roaring Brook Press
New York

For Kerry, Cory, and Nicole

Published by Roaring Brook Press

Roaring Brook Press is a division of Holtzbrinck Publishing Holdings Limited Partnership

120 Broadway, New York, NY 10271

mackids.com

Library of Congress Control Number: 2019932583

ISBN 978-1-250-14711-0

Our books may be purchased in bulk for promotional, educational, or business use. Please
contact your local bookseller or the Macmillan Corporate and Premium Sales Department at (800) 221-7945
ext. 5442 or by email at MacmillanSpecialMarkets@macmillan.com.

First edition, 2019

Book design by Monique Sterling

Printed in China by Toppan Leefung Printing Ltd., Dongguan City, Guangdong Province

1 3 5 7 9 10 8 6 4 2

Contents

Prologue
A Horrible, Hot Night

The South American country of Ecuador straddles the Andes mountain chain like a Band-Aid stretched over a knuckle. The capital city of Quito sits high on the knuckle (9,300 feet elevation), and a braided chain of bus routes threads north–south along the rugged mountain backbone, weaving in between towering volcanic peaks and a string of little cities connecting Quito with Colombia to the north and Peru to the south. The country plunges downward on either side of this backbone, steep mountainsides covered with cloud forest dropping to the scorching Pacific coast to the west, and into the sweltering Amazon basin to the east.

Chimborazo volcano, Ecuador, 1991.

Lita was next on my list. I'd already been to seven other towns in Ecuador in my search for rhinoceros beetles, and I had yet to find even a single beetle. A small tangle of buildings clinging to the mountainside, Lita was at just the right elevation for the beetles, and my guidebook assured me there would be both electricity and a little *pension*—hotel—where I could stay. Even better, I could take a tiny train to get there. Apparently, a single track connected Ibarra in the high Andes with San Lorenzo on the coast, and Lita was a whistle-stop roughly halfway in between. The view was supposed to be spectacular.

After a dusty bus ride from Quito to Ibarra, I discovered that the "train" was really just a bus that had been fitted with special wheels to ride on rails. (I guess that's why they called it a *"ferroBUS"* instead of a *"ferroCARRIL."*) And it only ran every other day. The tiny train/bus shuttled people down from the mountains to the coast on one day, and then climbed all the way back up to Ibarra on the next. I had just missed it, so my choice was to sit tight for two days or find another ride.

I'm not great at sitting still. I asked around at the market and found out about *camionetas*—large pickup trucks with high-sided wooden backs that look a bit like giant fruit crates on wheels. I found a driver heading for Lita that afternoon and climbed aboard. Twenty other people were already piled inside, so I set my backpack in a corner and squatted beside it on the floor, surrounded by sweaty bodies and bags of produce, clothes, and blankets, as well as a half-dozen chickens and a small pig. Gears scraped, the truck lurched, and we were off on our eight-hour drive to Lita.

By about 9:30 that night, all but one family had gotten off. We continued to bounce along in the darkness for another half hour before the truck stopped and the driver came around back to explain to us that the road was washed out. He was going no farther. "How far is Lita?" I asked. *"Lejos."* Far.

Curious kids on my trip to Lita.

So there I was, twenty-three years old, traveling by myself in a strange land, scared and stranded in the dark in the middle of nowhere. By that point we had dropped in elevation enough that it was hot. The air felt thick like steam. It was hard to breathe and I'd started to sweat. The family included three very young kids (*gua-guas*), and they had a ridiculous amount of supplies crammed into an assortment of plastic and burlap bags. There was no way they could carry all their stuff, so I strapped what I could to my already heavy backpack, put a burlap bag full of wool blankets on my shoulders, and took another bag full of pots and pans in my free hand. We started walking.

For five hours we stumbled through the sticky darkness, until we came at last to the house of the cousin of the father. He had a car, but the headlights were broken and we'd have to wait until morning to continue our journey. I was ready to drop from exhaustion and asked if there was water "to drink"—as in, sterilized or boiled. They produced a greasy plastic gas can and we all drank in the candlelight. They showed me to a wooden floor in a shed where I unfurled my sleeping bag.

Tap, tap, tap. Tap, tap. I woke at first light face-to-face with a chicken. Then I panicked a bit when I discovered the source of the water we'd drunk in the dark the night before. They handed me the now-empty gas can and pointed to a river. This was not the first river I'd drunk from in Ecuador, but it was definitely the dirtiest—red-brown sludge gliding through a cattle pasture.

The cousin's car was broken, but the neighbor had a truck and we bounced at last into Lita eighteen hours after setting out from Ibarra. I searched the surrounding forest for beetles and learned all I needed to know by midmorning the next day. This town, like all the others, wasn't going to work. I wouldn't find my beetles here.

At least for my return I got to ride on the train. The little *ferrobus* was already overflowing with people when it rolled into Lita, so

I climbed up onto the roof. The view was—as my guidebook had promised—incredible.

My name is Doug Emlen. I'm a scientist and I study beetles. Actually, to be precise, I don't just study beetles. What I really study are *weapons*—BIG weapons like antlers, horns, and tusks—and the particular weapons I work on happen to belong to beetles.

PART 1

Finding the Right Beetle

CHAPTER 1

My Mystery

I was going to solve a mystery.

For as long as I can remember I've been obsessed with big weapons. From mastodons with curling tusks to triceratops with five-foot-long horns, if it had a weapon attached to its body, I needed to know more about it. In every room at the natural history museum loomed another species with a crazy protrusion jutting from its head, or from between the shoulder blades, or from the end of its tail. Gallic moose with twelve-foot-wide antlers and arsinotheres with horns six feet long and a foot wide at the base. I couldn't peel my eyes from these creatures.

Why were their weapons so big?

As I grew and began to study biology, I realized that "big" had little to do with absolute size. Extreme weapons were all about proportion. Some of the most magnificent structures are borne by tiny creatures. Hiding in drawer after drawer of dried, pinned insects in museum archives, for example, are uncountable numbers of oddball species;

Bull elk with antlers.

beetles with front legs so long they have to be folded awkwardly around the animal in order to shut the lid on the case, or horns so big the animals have to be mounted in the drawer sideways. Many species are so small that their weapons only become apparent with a microscope: twisted tusks protruding from the faces of West African wasps, for example, or broad, branched antlers adorning the faces of flies.

Given that most animals don't have much in the way of weapons at all, why do a few species have weapons—the antlers of moose or tusks of mammoths, for example—that get really, really big? What's so special about these particular species? Why do *their* weapons get huge, while weapons in related species stay small?

I began my career determined to study extreme weapons, so I set out to find the craziest, most bizarre animals that I could. I also wanted my research to take me someplace exotic. In my case, this meant the tropics, so I narrowed my search.

All told, the animals I wanted to study needed to:

- Have a really big weapon
- Live in an exciting (preferably tropical) place
- Be easy to find in large numbers
- Be easy to observe in the wild, and
- Be easy to rear in captivity

Woolly mammoth tusks.

As fate would have it, the animals that best fit this bill were beetles, and the most promising species lived in South America.

Beetles are much smaller than moose or mammoths but relative to their body size, their weapons can still be massive. Typically, in beetle species males are the ones that grow horns. Beetle horns stick out from their bodies in awkward ways—some are short and stubby, flat wedges jutting up from the beetle's back, while others are long and slender, reaching in front of the beetle like a medieval knight's jousting lance. Some horns work like pincers, others like crowbars, and still others like fencing sabers. There are beetle horns that branch into a shovel-like pitchfork in front of a male's face, and horns that, when not in use, wrap neatly around the beetle body, ready to be flipped forward for combat simply by dipping the head.

Dynastes hercules, a "rhinoceros" beetle with pincer-like horns. The underside of the top horn is covered with delicate orange hairs.

Trypoxylus dichotomus,
a rhino beetle with a
pitchfork-shaped horn.

Depending on the species, beetle horns can be smooth, ridged, or studded with teeth; some are even sheathed in rows of orange hairs. Collectively, the diversity of beetle horns is unmatched in animal arsenals, with thousands of different species sporting horns of one sort or another, and many species having two, three, or even five different horn types. Not even the antlers of elk and moose can match the extraordinary range of shapes of beetle horns.

Beetle horns outmatch antlers in another way too. They're bigger than antlers, at least from the perspective of the males that grow and carry them. Consider a bull elk, for example. The largest bulls weigh almost eight hundred pounds, and they carry an impressive pair of weapons: bony beams sprouting from the base of the skull that extend more than four feet apiece and branch into as many as six or seven tines. Together, a pair of elk antlers can weigh more than forty pounds. This means bulls spend most of their life carrying *forty pounds* of bone on the top of their head—5 percent of a bull's total body weight.

Beetle horns get even bigger. The largest beetle horns can weigh as much as 30 percent of a male's body. I'd have to carry a fifty-pound sack of dog food on my head to compare, or, better yet, a coffee table. Try going about your daily business with an upside-down coffee table stuck to your skull. That's how big these weapons are, once you consider them from the perspective of the beetle.

Fiddler crabs look like they should tip over, their weapons are so big.

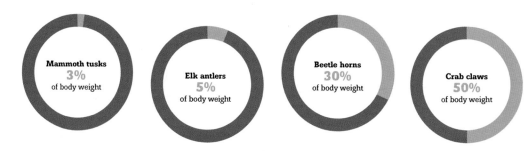

How big are the biggest weapons? Males in a number of species invest a lot in their weapons. This can be expressed as a percent of their total body weight. Elk antlers, for example, top out at 5% of the weight of the largest bulls. Relative to their body size, beetle horns are even bigger. These can be up to 30% of a male's body weight. The record holder for the biggest weapons of all goes to the fiddler crab, where claws in the largest males weigh as much as all the rest of his body combined. These males really should tip over!

Charles Darwin, the famous nineteenth-century naturalist, once stated: "From the small size of insects, we are apt to undervalue their appearance. If we could imagine a male *Chalcosoma* [rhinoceros beetle] with its polished, bronzed coat of mail, and vast complex horns, magnified to the size of a horse or even of a dog, it would be one of the most imposing animals in the world."

Darwin wrote that phrase more than one hundred years ago, and yet, by the 1990s, we still knew almost nothing about the biology of beetle horns. More than a thousand different dung beetle species have horns, for example, and not one of them had been examined in detail. Most people didn't even know these weapons existed, much less what they were used for, why they were so huge, or why they were so diverse from species to species.

This was now my mystery to solve.

Darwin's rhinoceros beetle, *Chalcosoma atlas.*

CHAPTER 2

The Plan

I set my sights on a species of rhinoceros beetle called *Golofa porteri*: handsome, coffee-colored scarabs the size of chicken eggs with two-inch-long horns sprouting like pincers from the head and shoulders of the males. *Golofa porteri* was listed as "common" in written accounts of its occurrence, and unlike most other rhinoceros beetle species, these animals did not live up in the tops of trees. Instead, they clung to bamboo shoots low to the ground where I could catch and observe them.

Before I could explain why only some species had horns, I needed to see how the horns were used. My plan had two parts:

First, I was going to study the behavior of a species with huge weapons (*Golofa porteri*) to see what the males did with their pincer-like horns.

Then I was going to compare this behavior to that of a second species, a close relative without weapons.

This would show me what was special about the biology or

Golofa porteri, my Ecuador species.

behavior of the beetles with horns and help me develop ideas for what, specifically, drove the evolution of these weapons.

Ecuador contains a second species of rhinoceros beetle called *Golofa unicolor,* which was perfect for comparing with *Golofa porteri* since the males look almost the same but lack horns. First, however, I needed to find the beetles with weapons.

So I headed to the heart of the beetles' range: the clouded slopes high on the sides of the Andes Mountains in Ecuador. Arriving in the capital city of Quito in August, I spent my first month immersed in a crash course in Spanish. For eight hours a day I worked one-on-one with my *professora,* practicing spelling and grammar and pronunciation. At night I stayed with an Ecuadoran family who spoke no English. Full immersion was exhausting, but it worked. After three weeks I was chatting with taxi drivers, and by the end of the fourth week I was ready to head off into the countryside.

The largest males have long pincer-like horns.

Map in hand, I started tracking down locations where I knew the beetles had been collected before.

In Pasochoa, Santo Domingo de los Colorados, Mindo, Baeza, Chiriboga, Nanegal, Riobamba, Baños, and Lita, I searched the cloud forests in vain. Now it looked like I was going to have to cross over into Colombia to find my beetles, and that was worrisome. It was 1990 and Colombia was still racked with poverty and crime, collateral damage from the ongoing war on drugs as the US attempted to halt the production and distribution of cocaine. I'd been told the place I was headed was well outside of the "war zone"—like going to Nebraska when there was fighting in Texas. "No problem!" Nevertheless, I was nervous.

Morning in the high Andes, Ecuador.

Red tile roofs typical of houses in the Andes.

CHAPTER 3

Men with Machetes

You have to actually walk across the border to get into Colombia. The taxi drivers all know both sides well, but they won't cross. So you get off at a bridge on one side, get your exit stamp in your passport, grab your gear and documents, walk across the bridge, go through the little customs office to get your entry stamp, and then pick up another taxi on the other side. In my case, however, there was a problem. The taxis on the other side wouldn't take me where I needed to go.

The road I needed—the main road connecting Ipiales and Tumaco—was under construction and traffic was allowed only at night. I was still nervous about traveling in Colombia, and even my guidebook warned never to go out at night. Yet there appeared to be no other way to get where I was going. None of the buses or taxis would take me during the daytime.

The problem was that the field station La Planada was six miles off the main road, on a dirt track that left the highway at the tiny town of Chucunés. The place was much too small to have a *pension*—it had just one little store, which would be closed in the middle of the night—and that meant finding a place to stay was going to be impossible.

So I tried my luck the next morning, ignoring what the officials had told me. Surely, somebody was going to be driving up that road during the day. I hired a taxi to take me as far as he could, an hour north of Ipiales to the turnoff where the road began heading west to Tumaco, and I got out and waited, hoping somebody would pass by. Two hours later a car finally arrived—a taxi, in fact—and the driver stopped and offered me a lift. I realized as soon as the door shut that I'd done exactly what my guidebook said never to do in Colombia. I'd gotten into a taxi already full with three men. Apparently, this was a fairly routine method for robbery—a driver with two other male "passengers." But these guys turned out to be really friendly, as did, for the record, all of the people I met in Colombia.

I was dropped off at the intersection—the only intersection—in Chucunés, and two men walking by offered to show me the way. They were heading up the mountain anyway. So off we went, they with machetes, hats, and small bags of rice and fruit, and me, the "outsider," hauling a full internal-frame backpack and a car battery for good measure (to power a backlight for attracting beetles at night).

The track zigzagged up the side of the mountain, a vertical climb of almost three thousand feet. And it was hot. Just placing one foot in front of the other was tough, and in my exhaustion, I soon became dangerously oblivious to everything around me.

Two-thirds of the way up my guides veered off the road onto a shortcut—an "indian trail" they called it—which was even steeper than the road because it dispensed with the zigzags. The trail pushed through a thick field of sugarcane, plants arching way over my head so that we were completely out of sight of the road. Once again, I'd put myself in a very bad spot: a tourist, walking exhausted and

Cloud forest near La Planada, Colombia: Perfect habitat for *Golofa* beetles.

heavily loaded with gear, away from all other people and flanked on each side by strangers wielding machetes. But what started out scary ended up being delicious. They cut stalks of sugarcane and we sucked the sticky liquid as we hiked. I drank directly from yet another river—I'd lost count by this point—and three hours later stumbled, at last, into "La Planada."

La Planada was a dream, a surreal oasis nestled in the cloud forest of the high Andes. The director, a Harvard-educated Colombian biologist who spoke better English than I did, met me at the door with a pitcher of iced tea and showed me into a dining hall replete with a full-spread buffet lunch. Awesome. As he showed me around the facility, I was speechless. There were well-maintained trails, laboratories with microscopes, research collections of local plants, a huge house with a veranda and hammocks, and dormitories with private bathrooms! The station offered three meals a day prepared by excellent chefs, and cost a mere $10 per night for scientists.

At last, a beetle!

Most important, though, La Planada had one thing none of the other places had. I finally found a beetle.

CHAPTER 4

Switching Species

My first attempt at beetle research was a bust. "Common," apparently, was open to interpretation—or at least to the whims of year-to-year changes in rainfall. Village after village, I bussed or trekked to a dozen possible study sites, to no avail. In the shadow of looming volcanoes, majestic cones soaring twenty thousand feet into the stark blue sky, I walked through mud streets bordered by brick-and-red-ceramic-tile houses carrying pictures of the beetles. Kids flocked to my side, pulling my sleeves, leading me to bamboo at the outskirts of the towns. But none of them knew the beetles. I circled beneath streetlights, hoping beetles might be drawn in by the glare.

Nothing. *Nada.* Weeks passed, and then months, as I ticked off each little town on my list. I'd ventured all the way into southern Colombia before I finally saw my first rhinoceros beetle in the wild. High on a mountain ridge choked with fog, I, at last, encountered a beetle. One beetle. A male, clinging to his bamboo stem, perched above the valley below.

One beetle was not even close to enough for my studies, and by the time I finally returned to Quito, out of both money and time, I'd managed to locate only thirteen.

Needless to say, my professors were not thrilled with my progress when I reported back to them at the end of the semester. Their verdict: Begin again. I needed a new species, one that really was common, and much easier to find. I knew what I needed to do. I'd been presented with the answer on my trip back to the States—another type of beetle that really *did* check all my boxes—I just didn't want to do it.

Phanaeus, a dung beetle with horns.

On my flight back from Ecuador I'd stopped for a few days in Costa Rica to visit a biologist and hero of mine, someone who'd spent his life studying tropical insects. His name is William Eberhard, and he had the solution to my problem: a type of beetle far more practical than *Golofa*. He flipped open the lid on a box full of specimens, all pinned neatly and lined up in little rows, and the stench smacked me like a slap to the face. I stepped back, eyes watering. "Those are *dung* beetles," I said. "There's no way I'm going to study dung beetles!"

But I was being foolish. He knew it. And, eventually, I knew it too. For the questions I wanted to ask, dung beetles were perfect. They have fantastic weapons; they live all over the world, including in the tropics; they can be observed in the wild and reared in the lab; and,

On my way to a Panama rain forest in search of dung beetles with horns.

most important of all, they really are common. They come tumbling into their food by the dozens, and sometimes even by the hundreds or thousands.

So now, at last, here I was, water splashing my face as the little boat sped across the Panama Canal toward a field station on an island teeming with dung beetles. Two huge duffel bags filled the seats behind me, bursting with clothes and gear—supplies that would last me almost eight months as I set up shop and began my beetle studies in the rain forest.

Red roofs of the Barro Colorado Island research station peek through the tropical forest.

There are lots of kinds of beetle. In fact, by some estimates, one out of every four species on the planet is a beetle. But within the beetles there are many different groups, ranging, for example, from whirligig beetles, to weevils, tiger beetles, rove beetles, bark beetles, and soldier beetles.

The beetles I study are all scarab beetles, a group that includes the flower beetles, June beetles, stag beetles, dung beetles, and rhinoceros beetles. Within the scarabs, there are several very clear and distinct lineages, all representing separate "families" within the overarching group of scarabs. Most of these groups lack dramatic weapons, but three of them are notorious for the armaments of their males. Stag beetles fight with oversized mouthparts, or mandibles, and in extreme cases these mandibles can be as long or longer than the rest of the body of the male. The other two families of scarabs have "horns"—rigid protrusions of the outer body wall (insects have their skeletons on the outside of their body, much like the suits of armor worn by medieval knights). One family, the rhinoceros beetles, includes species that feed primarily on decaying vegetation and plant roots; these were the critters I'd tried and failed to find in Ecuador. The other family, the dung beetles, feeds, well, on animal dung.

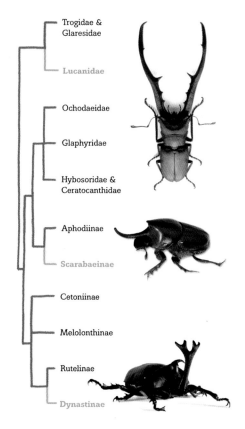

Family tree for the scarab beetles showing the stag beetles (Lucanidae), the dung beetles (Scarabaeinae), and the rhinoceros beetles (Dynastinae).

PART 2

Figuring Out Why
Beetles Have Horns

CHAPTER 5

A Fresh Start

What an incredible place!

Barro Colorado is an island with a mini-village built for scientists. A Panamanian crew of carpenters, cooks, and office administrators arrived every morning by boat, worked for the day, and departed again at the end of the afternoon, returning to their homes and families on the mainland. The rest of the population was made up of scientists. Occasionally, a professor would visit for a few weeks, but most of the biologists in residence were students just like me—aspiring researchers in their late teens or early twenties—and after the crews left for the day we had the whole island to ourselves.

My dorm room was on the upstairs floor of a rickety old laboratory called Chapman Lab, which was part of a cluster of rundown buildings collectively known as the "old lab." Most of the scientists lived in a suite of freshly painted concrete dormitories adjacent to the offices and dining hall below, close to the docks and the water. Only a few of us stayed at the top of the hill in the old buildings.

The Barro Colorado Island facility and harbor was a gateway to the tropical forest. Chapman Lab and swimming raft are indicated with arrows.

But I preferred it up here, at the crest of a winding concrete path of more than two hundred steep steps. It was wilder, and the forest felt so much closer.

Chapman Lab perched right at the edge of a steep slope and was surrounded by thick forest. A row of tall windows wrapped all the way around three sides of my room and, since it was hot, these windows were permanently open—there wasn't even any glass—only mesh screening. Breezes flowed straight through the room. When it

Some of the stairs leading up to the "old lab."

Chapman Lab, with its screened-in permanently open windows. My room at the far end (out of sight) was surrounded on three sides by screens.

poured, which it did a lot, thick mist drifted in through the screens, moistening my desk and the sheets of my bed. The canopies of nearby trees were so close that branches scratched against the screens and colorful birds chattered as they fed on eye-level fruits mere feet from my desk.

At night I'd lie there, covered only with a thin sheet, ceiling fan softly whirring, and close my eyes and listen. The rain forest came alive at night, almost purring with sound. A dozen types of tree cricket chirped. Bullfrogs groaned and giant toads whined. Tiny tungara frogs guarded territories in a puddle directly beneath my windows, and they sang for most of every night. Tinamous—secretive, chicken-sized birds—hooted an eerie, resonant trill. This rich tapestry of noise floated over an ever-present pitter-patter of water, dripping from the trees overhead, splattering on branches and leaves as it fell, punctuated only by the deafening roar of a downpour.

About twenty of us were here for "the long haul"—that is, stints in residence of six months or longer—and we grew to be close friends. Life settled into a routine. There'd be gatherings in the evenings in a little lounge where we made cookies in the kitchenette and played games. Some nights, when the sky was clear, we'd canoe to a little raft in the bay and float in the darkness under the stars. We always had to scan for eyeshine with our flashlights first, to make sure there were no caimans, before we dared dive into the cool water in the moonlight.

Each night this forest would "come alive" with sound.

Our days slid into a rhythm of work: designing experiments, collecting data, analyzing data, rethinking the experiments when they didn't work, and starting the process all over again. Design, execute,

Early light in the understory.

analyze, solve the problem, repeat. This was the humdrum reality of learning to do research in the maze of a tropical forest. Climb trees, measure leaves, trap squirrels, count seeds, or whatever each of our respective projects required. For me, my days always began with monkeys.

My alarm chirped at 5:00 A.M. and I sat up in bed, listening in the darkness for the guttural scream of the howlers. There were at least fifteen different extended-family groups, or troops, of howler monkeys spread out across the island, and each morning like clockwork the dominant male of each troop announced his location to rivals in adjacent territories. When the monkeys were nearby, their howls were so loud they hurt. But those were good mornings because I could find the monkeys and beetles quickly. On other mornings the dawn cries were just barely discernible above the din of the forest night, and I might have a mile or more to hike before I found them. My routine was simple: Use a compass to mark the direction of the sound, and then go back to sleep. An hour later, when it was actually starting to get light inside the forest, I'd head into the understory mist and follow my compass to track down that day's troop.

The rain forest glittered this morning, sun streaking through cracks in the canopy trapping clouds of steam in angled slabs of blinding light. Millions of raindrops clung to leaves and sparkled. After my eyes adjusted, I headed out on established trails, sticking

An agouti stares at me as I head off the trail, tracking the monkeys.

I found them! Howlers watch from above as I go about my work.

to them as far as I could before weaving into the understory, over vines and around trees as I jogged toward the now-silent monkeys, guided only by my compass. All the while, I was listening for movement—any movement—in the canopy above. A branch rattled, then a snap. I had them. Dark faces glared down at me, coal-black shadows against the leaves.

Once I found the monkeys it was a quick task to find the dung, and it never took long for the beetles to arrive. Big, shiny, metallic beetles landed with a plunk and clambered over twigs and leaves. Tiny yellow-and-brown beetles perched on leaves with their antennae outstretched, reaching for scent. Within minutes beetles were everywhere, flying back and forth in tiny sweeps as they maneuvered clumsily into the pieces of fallen dung. Soon, still other pea-sized beetles zigzagged over to the dung fragments (they really fly in a "zigzag," not a straight line). Swirls of flies landed first on surrounding leaves before hopping onto the dung as well. In less than an hour the forest swarmed with insects that had all converged on the dung to find food and mates.

The species I was after, called *Onthophagus acuminatus,* has no common name and is rarely noticed by anyone other than entomologists. I chose them because the largest males sport a pair of impressive horns, two cylindrical rods jutting up from the back of their head, making them look, I thought, like miniature versions of the dinosaur *Triceratops.* Smaller males are hornless—they develop with only nubbins where the weapons would be—and none of the females have horns.

On a good morning I could gather as many as a hundred of the little beetles—much better yields than I'd gotten while searching for the elusive Ecuadoran *Golofa*—and I could fill a Ziploc bag with howler monkey dung, their food. I'd bring all of this back to the main laboratory, where I had a system set up to measure the horns under a microscope, and where I kept colonies of the beetles in containers filled with moist soil, ready for experiments.

All dung beetles have a problem. The food they feed on is precious—high quality and hard to find. (I know, it's hard for us to imagine poop as precious—but as far as insect diets go, it's about as good as they come.) Unlike plant leaves, for example, dung is loaded with vital nutrients like protein that larvae need to grow. Lots of insects love to feed on dung. The problem is that *too* many insects want it, and dung disappears fast.

Dung beetles are famous for their exquisite sense of smell. They don't have noses, like we do, and instead smell with their antennae. Beetle antennae are tuned to the particular smells that matter most for each species, and for dung beetles this means the odors of dung. By following plumes of scent, beetles converge on fresh dung, often arriving just minutes after it appears. Getting there first is one way to beat the competition. But even this is not enough, and when they get there, beetles almost always have to contend with tons of other insects. Lots of species all come in for their share of the prize.

Dung beetles deploy one of two strategies to fend off other insects. Some species, called "rollers," carve big chunks of dung into a ball and push it away from the pile. In this way, they can cover a lot of ground fast and hide their ball away from the rest of the crowd. Other species, called "tunnelers," pull dung away from the pile in a different direction: down. These beetles—including my focal species—don't carve off a big piece all at once. Instead, by digging a tunnel directly beneath the dung, these beetles can stash lots of little pieces one after the other. They make hundreds of trips, pulling dung into their burrow where other insects can't get it. Both ball rollers and tunnelers solve the problem of competition for their food; they just do it in different ways.

CHAPTER 6

Peeking into Tunnels

Before heading to Panama I'd driven to Ottawa, Canada, to meet with the leading expert on dung beetles. Henry Howden had traveled the world collecting beetles, pinning hundreds of thousands of specimens for the Canadian Museum of Nature. He let me study his personal collection, and he taught me how to tell apart the different species I was likely to find on Barro Colorado Island. He even gave me a few beetles to take with me, so I could be sure I knew who was who.

I remember him telling me "No, the males don't use their horns in fights." I was astonished, for I absolutely expected to find that dung beetle horns decided the outcomes of battles between rival males. After all, the horns were confined to the males in these species (if they served some other purpose, say, for example, to make the beetle more difficult for a predator to swallow, then why wouldn't females have them too?). And in all the other species with male weapons—things like caribou, fiddler crabs, elephants, and ibex— weapons clearly functioned in male battles for access to females.

But Henry was the world expert. He'd collected beetles from all over the globe, and, in the process of collecting, he'd had plenty of opportunities to watch them. The pattern, he said, was backwards. The species with big horns almost never fight. They clamber right past each other, in some cases even stepping on another beetle's face, without eliciting so much as a shove from a rival male. Species without horns, on the other hand, fight all the time. These hornless species are easy to watch. Males carve little balls of dung and roll them away from the pile, and, as they do, they get trounced by rivals. Males plow into each other from all sides, pulling and twisting in a tangle. These "ball-rolling" species are the fighters, he said, and they never have horns. How could horns function for battle if the fighting species *don't* have them, and the nonfighting species *do*?

Henry's words stayed with me as I began my work in Panama. Here was another riddle I was going to have to solve. Thanks to Henry, I knew I needed to watch these beetles very closely, to observe them doing whatever it was that they did. In particular, I had to figure out what the horned species were doing with their horns.

Canthon angustatus, a ball-rolling Panama dung beetle.

Although ball-rolling beetles fight all the time, they never have horns.

Into the forest I went, tracking the monkeys and finding their dung. I got there as soon as the dung fell from the trees and set up shop. Clipboard in hand and a camera beside me, I waited for the beetles to arrive.

In they came. Just like Henry had foretold, the ball rollers showed up in droves, carving little spheres of dung and pushing them away from the crowd. Rivals pounced, and males ended up in writhing tangles. Often two or three additional males would arrive, and they'd

Tunneling beetles like this one, on the other hand, often do have horns.

push into the tussle too. Eventually, one of the males would win, and continue pushing his marble-sized ball of dung. Sometimes the ball would get ripped apart in the midst of battle, and two males would each push lopsided halves along opposite paths.

Clearly, these ball-rolling beetles were fighters, just as Henry had predicted, and none of them had horns. His other observation held true too. At least five different species here had horns, and these guys ignored one another. No fighting at all! They'd waddle right over each other, oblivious of other beetles, and then disappear into an underground tunnel. Here were the beetles with the big weapons—including my focal species with magnificent horns—and nobody seemed to be doing anything interesting, weapon-wise. The

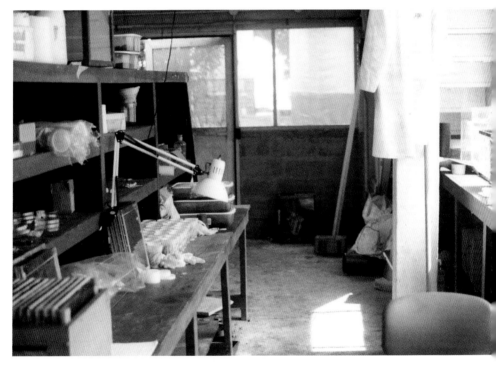

My lab on Barro Colorado Island, with glass-sided "beetle farms" on the counter to the left. (Yes, it often was a mess, but I *was* working with dirt and dung beetles, after all!)

problem was, once they plunged into the blackness of a tunnel, I couldn't watch them anymore. In fact, once they vanished into their tunnels, nobody knew what they did.

A century earlier, the French naturalist Jean-Henri Fabre tried to watch what happened inside dung beetle tunnels. He cut a hole in the bottom of a pie tray and mounted it on top of a long glass tube filled with moist soil. When his beetle pairs burrowed belowground, they did so inside the glass cylinder. He was able to catch glimpses of their mating and parenting behavior in places where the sides of their tunnel came up against the glass.

But Fabre wasn't interested in weapons, and he never placed more than one male and one female in his chambers. So, while he saw incredible examples of parents tending to their eggs, he witnessed not one single fight.

During my first fall on Barro Colorado Island I built "beetle farms"—glass-and-soil sandwiches that I propped up on end—to watch what happened underground. On top I set a plastic bin with a slit cut in the floor, lined up precisely so that the glass sides of my beetle farm fit snugly into the slot, flush with the floor of the bin. I placed monkey

Watching what happens inside tunnels, using "beetle farms" and red-filtered light.

dung in the center, right over the soil strip, and introduced beetles—colored dots painted on their backs so I could tell them apart.

It didn't work. The beetles burrowed into the soil just fine, but they hated the bright lights I was using to watch them. After all, natural tunnels are completely dark, and I guess blinding light shining in from the side distracted them. So I purchased bolts of heavy black cloth in Panama City and rigged a giant tent inside my lab. I draped the thick fabric from the ceiling so that it fell over my head and behind the chambers, placing all of the beetle farms in total darkness. Then I did something really clever. I can't take credit for this idea—others had used it before me—but I exploited the fact that most insects see the world very differently from us. They can see ultraviolet light (UV), for example, which we cannot. And we can see red light, which they cannot. Beetle eyes cannot detect red light. I set my beetle farms in a row and propped up several powerful floodlights with red filters taped over the lenses. My cloth cave glowed red, giving me enough light to see them. At long last I could watch what the beetles did.

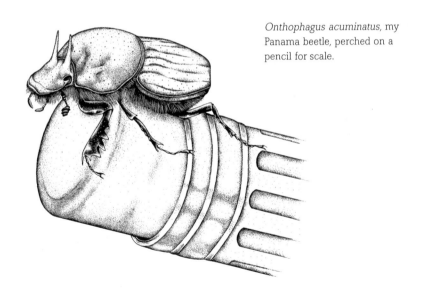

Onthophagus acuminatus, my Panama beetle, perched on a pencil for scale.

CHAPTER 7

Beetle Battles

They did a lot! The beauty of this design was that I could replicate my observations, setting up chamber after chamber and watching hundreds of beetles go through their daily routine. This allowed me to identify clear patterns, and, after weeks and weeks of watching, I finally knew exactly how they behaved.

Females dug the tunnels. As soon as they arrived at the dung they plowed straight into the soil below. Like powerful little bulldozers, females scraped armfuls of clay and dirt, spun around, and then used their broad faces to push the loosened soil all the way up the tunnel to the surface. Spin back down, carve some more, eject the soil, repeat. In a matter of minutes, female beetles dug tunnels more than a foot deep into the soil beneath pieces of howler monkey dung.

Then began the real work. Once the tunnel was dug, it needed to be provided with food for the female's young. Trip after trip—I counted as many as fifty trips in an hour—the female would race up the tunnel to the dung, grab a piece, and, clenching it tightly in her jaws, pull it all the way down to the end of the tunnel. There, after chewing it carefully to remove debris (and possibly to kill any eggs laid by pesky flies who also feed on the dung), she'd pack it into the closed end of the tunnel. More than a hundred trips later she'd have assembled, piece by piece, a dense, pinky-sized "sausage" of dung crammed into the tip of the tunnel. At one end she carefully places a single egg. Then she gently seals off the egg, filling in the tunnel in front with a half inch of soil, before beginning the process all over again for a new egg.

One female could stash dung for as many as twenty eggs in succession, gradually filling in the tunnel behind her as she worked.

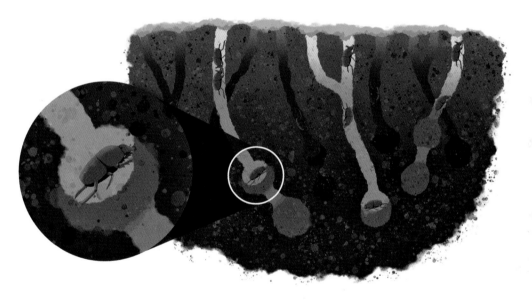

A busy female stashing food for her young.

A day in the life of a female beetle:
1. Dig tunnel
2. Pull dung into tunnel (~100 trips per brood ball)
3. Lay egg in brood ball
4. Repeat (5 to 20 brood balls per tunnel)

Her tunnel grew shorter as she packed it full of eggs. When she ran out of space, she'd simply carve a new shaft branching off from the original. By the end of this process her tunnel might include three or four winding forks, each studded with eggs and dung sausages like beads on a collection of strings, all of them merging into the single original tunnel entrance at the top.

While the females worked, males battled for possession of the tunnels. They weren't battling aboveground, but below! Like miniature

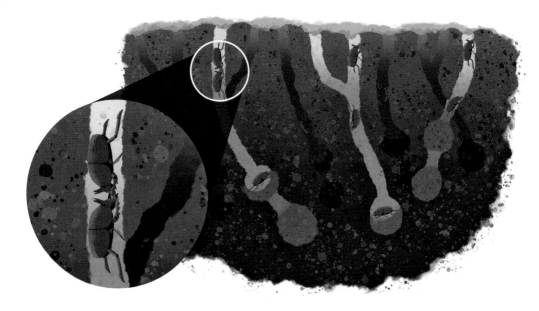

Males attempt to block the tunnel entrance, battling rival males that try to enter.

A day in the life of a male beetle:

1. Guard entrance from rivals

2. Fight with intruders who attempt to enter

3. Try to keep female from leaving tunnel

tanks, males planted themselves just inside the entrances, facing out, ready to challenge every rival male who attempted to enter. Many of the fights were quick, as outmatched intruders took stock and turned to leave. Other fights, particularly ones where the males were evenly matched, escalated into drawn-out brawls. Males locked horns and pushed, straining to supplant the other beetle. For the intruding male, the trick was to push past the guarding male, slipping into the tunnel below. Pulling this off gave *him* the advantage, for he could now brace against the walls and block, gradually forcing the original male up and out of the tunnel.

Some fights were so intense they degenerated into a whirling, shoving, tumble, with battling beetles retreating all the way to the bottom of the tunnel, crashing into the female, or bursting up and out the entrance onto the soil surface above. I was glad I'd painted distinguishing marks on the beetles beforehand, as these intense fights were impossible to follow. Beetles flipped past each other, switching position over and over, and I'd lose track of who was who. Eventually, however, even these fights ended, and I could tell from the paint marks on the beetle running away who had lost, and who had won. To the victor go the spoils, and in this case, the winning male would go down the tunnel to the female and mate with her. In fact, guarding males mated with the female inside their tunnel every few hours while she laid her eggs.

The males *did* fight—the big ones, at least—and the horns *were* used in battles between rival males. It turns out Henry Howden had been partly correct. Aboveground, dung beetles on Barro Colorado Island behaved just as he'd predicted they would. He just hadn't been able to see the whole story. For the species with horns, everything interesting was happening belowground.

Rival males pushed, pried, and twisted, straining with thick legs braced against tunnel walls, locking horns with opponents in fierce struggles for possession of the tunnel. In these fights, horn length

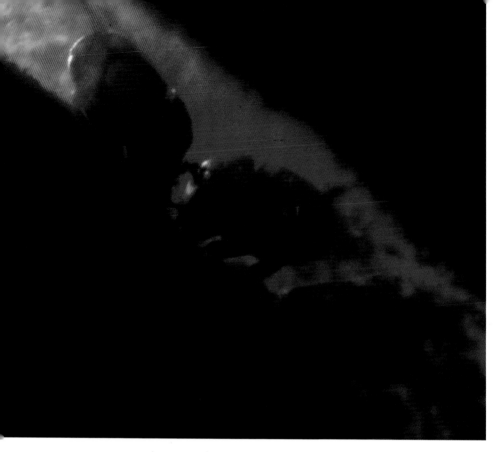

Battling beetles inside a tunnel. The female, busy packing dung into the end of the tunnel, is visible to the right.

mattered. Over and over, in fight after fight, the advantage went to the male with the larger weapons. In these beetles, as in so many other animal species with male weapons, the males with the biggest weapons won. Over time, weapons in populations like this will evolve to greater and greater extremes.

At last, I had the first piece to my puzzle. I now knew why males in my beetles had big weapons: They fought fights inside tunnels where horns gave males an edge. Males with the biggest weapons won, and this benefit to having long horns presumably pushed their populations into an escalating cycle of weapon evolution—an arms race. But the other half of my mystery revolved around the beetles without horns.

If horns were so great, then why didn't all of the dung beetles in the Panamanian forest have them?

Why did arms races get triggered in *tunneling* dung beetles but not in ball rollers?

If I wanted to explain the significance of huge weapons, I was going to have to figure out why some species get sucked into arms races, while so many others do not.

CHANGE OVER TIME, OR HOW AND WHY WEAPONS GET BIG

Imagine, for example, a population of antelope where the average length of male horns is four inches. A few males stand out: They have five-inch horns. These lucky few males win battles the most frequently; they mate with the greatest proportion of female antelope; and their offspring make up the majority of the next generation (including lots of sons with five-inch horns). These sons win fights too, since they've also got long horns, and their kids spread even more. Over the next few dozen generations the population shifts, as more and more males are born with horns that grow to be five inches. A gradual change like this, where the average size, shape, or color of an animal shifts from one generation to the next, is *evolution*.

Our antelope population just evolved from one where bucks had four-inch horns to one where most of them now have five-inch horns. But consider what happens next. The benefits of a five-inch horn aren't so great anymore, because everybody has horns this big. Now it takes an even bigger weapon to win. If a male in this population stumbled on a way to grow six-inch horns, he'd have the advantage. He'd win the fights and mate with the most females. His offspring—including sons inheriting six-inch horns—would outnumber the rest. A few dozen generations down the road the population will have shifted once again. Soon six-inch horns won't be so great, and it'll take a seven-incher to win. In this way, the size of a weapon can steadily increase, as bigger and bigger versions arise, spread, and replace their earlier and smaller counterparts. Seven-inch horns eventually give way to eight- and then nine-inch horns, and weapon sizes ratchet up to ever greater proportions.

When a particular subset of a population performs best—say the biggest individuals, or the ones with the longest horns—then the population experiences *selection*. The term selection comes from breeding practices. A farmer might select corn plants with the biggest kernels, or a dog breeder the pups with the friendliest temperaments. Breeding only individuals with the desired traits causes populations to evolve, so that over time these characteristics become more common.

In our antelope example—and in my Panamanian dung beetle—we can say that selection favors larger weapon sizes. Measure selection in the antelope population now, measure it in a decade, measure it a thousand years in the future, and we're likely to find the same thing: Males with the biggest horns win. The particular weapon size performing best will change (four-inch horns give way to five-inch horns, and then to six-inch horns, and so on), but the *direction of selection* remains constant. All else being equal, this form of selection is going to lead to an arms race, and the evolution of very big weapons!

VICIOUS CYCLES

Weapons like the ones I study get huge because they get caught up in an arms race. Arms races happen when populations of animals get locked into a back-and-forth cycle, a tornado of sorts, where each side experiences selection to match and then surpass the weapons of the other. One male and his descendants acquire a new and better weapon, giving them an edge in the contests. They begin to win, until another male manages to surpass it, at which point *he* and *his descendants* start to win. Back and forth these cycles go, leading to bigger, more elaborate, and more expensive weapons. On and on, weapons caught up in an arms race get bigger and bigger and bigger, until the race climaxes with structures of outlandish proportion and cost.

Weapons caught up in an arms race get sucked into a "vicious cycle" of escalation. This can drive the evolution of extreme weapon sizes.

PART 3

Figuring Out Why Most Species *Don't* Have Big Weapons

(Hint: Big Weapons Aren't Cheap)

CHAPTER 8

Making a Bigger Weapon

I was pretty sure now that I knew why big horns were benefi-cial to my beetles. They helped males win fights over females. And I was pretty sure that this process, carried over enough time, could drive the evolution of longer and longer horns. But why not test this idea directly?

Just as cattle ranchers can improve their herds by selectively breeding only bulls with the best characteristics, why couldn't I make longer horns by selectively breeding only the longest-horned males? In order to further understand how and why certain beetles grew horns, I decided it made sense to actually *watch* the beetle horns evolve. I planned to accomplish this in the dusty shed that served as my laboratory. I purchased in bulk ten-foot-tall bags of unlabeled plastic shampoo bottles from a company in Panama City. I cut the tops off each bottle so that they formed cylindrical tubes twelve inches deep and three inches in diameter. Almost a thousand of these tubes lined the counters of my little screened-in lab, each one filled with ten inches of packed, moist, sandy soil. An ice-cream scoop's worth of monkey dung sat at the top, and the whole thing was enclosed by screen mesh and a rubber band. A thousand furnished homes, if you happen to be a dung beetle.

Each tube would house a single pair of beetles, going about their business of pulling pieces of dung into a tunnel and forming them into brood balls. On the tip of each ball sat an egg, perched on a tiny stalk and encased in a thin shell of soil and dung. Once the egg hatched, the larva would spend the entirety of its development inside the little dung ball, eating and growing in solitude until it was ready to crawl to the soil surface as an adult a month later. Each pair of beetles could provision roughly six to eight of these egg-containing sausages in a week, and I kept them at it, giving them fresh dung every few days, until I had twenty or thirty offspring per pair.

I started with a hundred wild-caught beetles, half males and half females. I measured the males under a microscope and selected the five males with the longest horns to serve as breeders. Each chosen male was paired with two different females in succession. (I chose the females at random from within the lab population, since females don't have horns.) The mated females were housed in separate shampoo-bottle tubes, and from each I attempted to collect between twenty and thirty offspring. Ten reproductive females times thirty offspring each yields roughly three hundred new beetles per generation. Males of this second generation would be measured, and, as before, the five individual males with the longest horns relative to their body size would be selected as breeders. Each male would be paired with two females apiece, and their offspring would become the third generation of the experiment, and so on.

The logic of "artificial selection" experiments is pretty straightforward. In my case, my breeding program selected for increased horn length in generation after generation of the population. The empirical question then concerned whether or not the population evolved in response to this selection. Did the horns of males get longer with each successive generation?

Treatments in a scientific experiment need to be replicated, however, to minimize the possibility of arriving at results by chance. Populations shift gradually from generation to generation simply as a result of serendipity. Picture a large jar full of fifty different colors of jelly beans, all mixed together. Reach in and scoop out a thousand and, chances are, you will happen to include most, if not all, of the fifty original types. Some might be a bit better represented in your scoopfuls than they had been before, but these changes in flavor frequency are likely to be minor. The jelly beans in the new jar should resemble the blend of flavors that were present in the old jar.

If, instead, you scooped only five jelly beans from the original jar, and these then populated your new jar, they almost certainly would not be representative. Most of the original fifty flavors would be lost. If those five jelly beans were then replicated until the new jar was full, the total number of jelly beans might be similar to what was present before, but the blend of flavors would be drastically different. The jelly bean "population" would have evolved simply due to chance.

I was selecting only five individual males and ten females to breed each generation. This is a small sample, and it meant that some shift in the traits of my population could have occurred by chance. If, at the end of my experiment, the males in my artificially selected population had longer horns than before, I couldn't rule out the possibility that this was a spurious result due to chance.

To confirm my findings, I would have to do the whole thing again. If you have not one, but two separate populations, both experiencing directional artificial selection for longer horn lengths, and they both result at the end in males with longer horns, it's a much more compelling result. Random changes are not likely to occur in the same direction both times. Even better, add still more populations selected

Scooping just a few jelly beans out of the jar can result in big changes in the blend of colors simply due to chance.

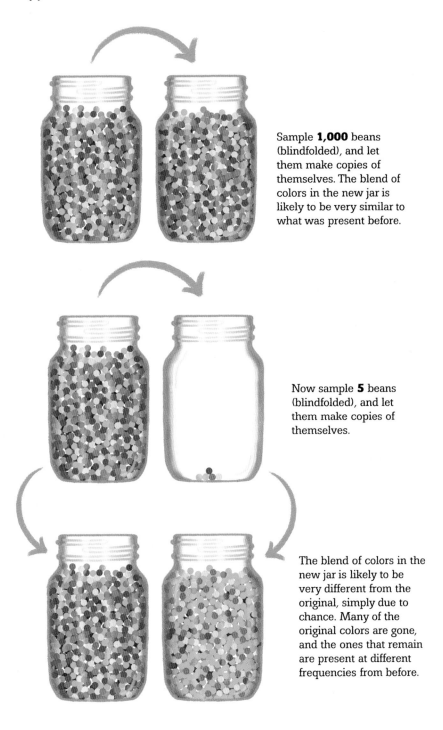

Sample **1,000** beans (blindfolded), and let them make copies of themselves. The blend of colors in the new jar is likely to be very similar to what was present before.

Now sample **5** beans (blindfolded), and let them make copies of themselves.

The blend of colors in the new jar is likely to be very different from the original, simply due to chance. Many of the original colors are gone, and the ones that remain are present at different frequencies from before.

Our population
evolved
simply due to
sampling error.

in the opposite direction—males with the shortest horns selected as the breeders—and keep them in the lab at the same time, feed them the same food, sample the same tiny number of individuals as breeders, and repeat the process for the same number of generations.

If several generations later we find that in both of the populations selected for long horns, males end up with longer horns than before, and in both of the populations selected for short horns, males have horns that are shorter than before, *then* we can begin to rule out chance. In fact, I conducted my experiment on six distinct populations of beetles simultaneously. In two of the populations I selectively bred only males with the longest horns; in two other populations I selectively bred only males with the shortest horns; and in the final two populations I chose the males at random. Keeping all these beetles supplied with food meant many, many mornings racing through the forest in search of monkeys. For *six hundred* sunrises I combed the damp understory, collecting bags of monkey dung to bring back to the lab so that I could feed the beetles in this huge experiment.

CHAPTER 9

Six Hundred Sunrises

Six hundred sunrises is a lot of time in the forest, and it gave me ample opportunity to learn my way around. One morning a silky anteater fell to the ground beside me, curled up into a furry ball the size of a grapefruit. When I picked up the stick she was clinging to she stuck out her long, squirming pink tongue, and I realized she had a tiny baby clinging to her back!

Another morning I stepped on a twig and heard a soft "whoosh." I was surrounded by a family of coatis—graceful, raccoon-like animals with long, bushy, striped tails. A mom and ten babies had all sprung at once to the nearest trees, and they clung there in a ring around me, each baby gripping a different trunk and glaring, tail twitching.

My favorite animals in the forest (besides beetles, of course) turned out to be the birds. For the first time in my life I began to appreciate birds. My dad is a biologist, and he's spent his whole life studying birds, answering questions like how indigo buntings use stars to find their way north when they migrate, or why white-fronted bee-eaters team up to raise their young. This year he was studying a bird that lived in Panama—a strange shorebird called the jacana that nested on a river about thirty miles away from Barro Colorado Island.

My grandfather was a biologist too, and even he studied birds—penguins in the Antarctic, and crows and quail. I'd grown up immersed in everything bird. I even thought it was normal to have dead buntings in little plastic bags stacked in the freezer next to the ice cream. But somehow it hadn't rubbed off on me. I'd never been excited by birds before—never wanted to go looking for them, and never bothered to learn one from another. Most telling of all, when it came time to choose my career path it was beetles, not birds, that inspired me.

Yet here in the forest I was surrounded. I could hear them everywhere I went, chattering and chirping and singing. As I worked with my beetles, on my hands and knees looking down at moist leaves and mud, I'd listen all the while to the sounds above—to the monkeys, to make sure they weren't maneuvering over my head to drop branches or try to pee on me—and to the birds too. I found that once I learned the calls of the pretty ones, they were so much easier to see. When a motmot or a trogon

Silky anteater clinging to her stick.

Coati clinging to a tree.

Keel-billed toucan in the Panama forest.

A crested guan visible through the branches.

perched above me, I'd *hear* them and I could take a break from what I was doing to look.

Antbirds followed army ant swarms, plucking grasshoppers and katydids from the masses of soldier ants, and male red-capped manakins buzzed and clicked in jittery dances to attract females in the

Leaf-mimicking mantis.

Rufous motmots, one of my favorite Panama birds, swish their tails back and forth like a clock pendulum.

understory. Keel-billed toucans squawked like squeaky sandals high overhead, and, each morning after sunrise, the forest rang with the calls of hundreds and hundreds of parrots, flying two by two across the treetops. The rain forest became my home as I got better and better at finding my way around "off-trail," and, especially, at finding monkeys.

Years later I would track beetles deep into Australia, poking under horse manure in leech-infested swamps with kangaroos. I'd dig for them in thick grasses on the high sides of Mauna Loa volcano on the Big Island of Hawaii, shivering in driving horizontal rain. I'd even search for them along the rim of Ngorongoro Crater in Tanzania. But I never got to "know" my surroundings—the smells and sounds and secrets—the way I did those years on Barro Colorado Island. There just isn't a substitute for time when it comes to understanding the biology around you.

JOURNAL ENTRY 1 *Too Many Ticks*

This morning the monkeys were not at all close to my room, and I had to hike an hour into the forest in search of dung. My first finds had all been tiny—not nearly enough to feed the hundreds of beetles now waiting in the lab. The problem with "false starts" such as these is that I only carry a pocketful of surgical gloves with me when I set out in the morning. At each collection spot I use one of the pairs of gloves to gather up the bits of monkey dung. After several insufficient stops I begin to run out of gloves. Mucking with monkey dung is unpleasant enough as it is; at least having disposable gloves leaves my hands clean and keeps dung off my lunch, water bottle, and binoculars.

Three miles from the lab and well into my last pair of gloves, I finally found the stash of dung that I needed. But as I was filling my bags I brushed against a palm frond covered with ticks. Any tropical biologist can tell you about "seed ticks," the bundles of babies (technically nymphs) that clump together on the tips of big leaves. Hundreds can pile together in a ball the size of a marble. Bump into them and they hurl themselves onto your body and begin to disperse. For this reason, standard forest garb is long pants tucked into socks, and a loose-fitting long-sleeved cotton shirt tucked into the pants. This works pretty well to keep stinging ants or tiny ticks from getting directly onto your skin. The other trick is to carry tape. Masking tape is best, and to keep it rapid-access most of us would stick several strips along our pants legs over our thighs. When we happened upon a ball of ticks we could grab the tape and use it to blot the babies off us in seconds, before they got past our clothing barrier.

My dilemma that morning was that I was on my last pair of gloves, and they had already started to tear. If I peeled them off I would never be able to get them back on again. I couldn't manage the tape with the gloves on, and I didn't want to harvest all the dung barehanded, so I ignored the ticks for the moment and finished filling my bags. It only took another five minutes or so before I was done but that was too long. I ripped the gloves off, grabbed the tape, and looked for the ticks. They were gone. In those few short minutes they'd dispersed across my body, and I couldn't find them.

The three-mile run back to the lab was agony. I could feel ticks crawling inside my shirt, down my legs, in my hair, behind my ears, even in my nose and around my eyes as I ran. I flung the dung bags into the lab and dashed to my room, jumping out of my clothes into a scalding and soapy shower, to no avail. They would not wash off. It took more than an hour with tweezers under an intense bright light to peel the ticks from my skin, plucking them from the places they'd lodged themselves and sticking them onto strips of tape like so many flecks of pepper. In the end I counted almost five hundred ticks on those clogged strips of tape.

A curious howler watches as I race to collect dung.

CHAPTER 10

Bigger Horns,
at a Price

Two years and seven beetle generations later, I had done it. The weapons had evolved. Males in populations selected for longer horns now sported weapons that were proportionately larger than they had been before, and males in populations selected for shorter horns had weapons that were proportionately smaller. Each of these extremes differed from the populations that had acted as controls, and I'd shown convincingly that animal weapons can evolve fast. But weapons weren't the only trait that changed; increases in horn size came at a price.

As weapons get big they also get expensive, and males with the longest horns now had stunted eyes. By the end of the experiment, males selected for longer horns had eyes that were 30 percent smaller than males selected for shorter horns. Stunted growth arises because of a limited availability of nutrients. Tissues require energy and materials to grow, and allocating resources to the production of one structure can mean that those same resources are no longer available for growth of another. Dung beetles were draining resources away from eyes in order to build bigger horns.

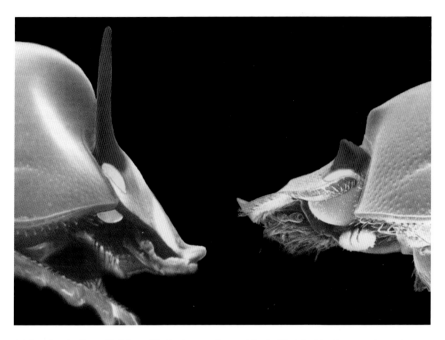

A big price for horns! Males with the longest horns (shaded in blue) had proportionately smaller eyes (shaded in yellow).

Males pay all sorts of crushing costs when their weapons get really big. Male fiddler crab claws, for example, are packed full of energy-burning muscle. Claws in the biggest males can double the weight of the male. This means the claw weighs as much by itself as all of the rest of the male's body combined (this is an animal that really should tip over). If I were a fiddler that would mean a 175-pound claw! But these claws don't just sit there, like a rigid beetle horn. They move. Males use them to squeeze their opponents when they fight, and even when they're not fighting, they wave them. Up and down, up and down, males hurl their claw up and drop it. Thousands of times a day, day after day, like blazing billboards advertising each male's ability to fight.

Claw muscles burn energy at an alarming rate even when resting, and constant waving costs quite a bit more. Not only do males burn through calories faster than females, but they feed more slowly, making it harder for them to recover these energy losses. Females have two feeding claws, delicate mouthparts that they use to pluck morsels of wet algae from grains of sand at the shoreline. Males have only one feeding claw, since the other is grossly enlarged into a weapon. They have twice the caloric demand, but only half of the feeding tools—not a great situation.

Male fiddler crabs have only one small mouthpart with which to feed, since the other claw is enlarged into a fighting weapon. Males wave their claws up and down, which is both energetically demanding and dangerous (since bright, moving claws are easy for predators to spot).

Crabs waving big claws also make obvious targets. Most predators cue in on movement, and brightly colored claws popping up and down are easy to spot. Also, as any lover of seafood well knows, crab claws are tasty. Not surprisingly, many predators prefer to feed on males with big claws, and, very often, male fiddlers get eaten before ever winning an opportunity to mate.

Moose, deer, and elk pay still other costs. In this case, the weapons—antlers—are made of bone, and bone is built from minerals like calcium and phosphorus. Bulls can't get enough of these minerals

Moose antlers are so expensive that bulls must leach minerals out of their other bones to make them.

from their diet, so they leach them out of the other bones in their skeleton. They shunt minerals from the rest of their bones into the growing antlers. This makes their skeleton brittle and fragile at precisely the time of year when bulls smash their bodies into rival bulls, locking antlers in dangerous struggles for dominance, increasing the chances that they break bones during the battle.

During "the rut," as this mating season is called, bulls fight battle after battle, in hundreds of contests, for opportunities to guard clustered groups of females. For the few victorious males, the reward is huge—a chance to breed with all of the females. For the rest of the males, the outcome is bleak. They pour resources into weapon growth and then starve themselves during weeks of expensive and dangerous battle. In the process, they get slashed and stabbed and stressed beyond measure, all in a doomed attempt to breed.

Big weapons are incredibly expensive.

Fallow deer battling for a chance to breed. For all but the biggest males, the prospects are bleak.

CHAPTER 11

Breaking the Rules

All the while as my breeding experiment unfolded in the shed, I continued setting up glass sandwiches, or beetle farms, in the cloth tent in my office and scrutinizing the behavior of the beetles. In chamber after chamber, I'd place two males and a female together to see what happened. Of course, what happened was fighting. Two males and one tunnel meant battles for possession. But there was a lot more going on than I at first realized.

After I'd watched enough of them, the fights became a blur, playing out the same way every time. Watching the winners wasn't very exciting. In the end, it was the losers who surprised me. If a big male lost a fight he'd storm off in search of another tunnel and another challenge. In my cages, he'd walk in endless circles around the edges of the Plexiglas boxes. But tiny males did something very different. After getting booted they'd only go a short distance away—maybe an inch—and there they'd begin to dig their own tunnel. Excavating tunnels is normally a *female* behavior, but here these little guys were making new tunnels, right beside the guarding males.

I got very excited when I first saw this, thinking the little male might sneak back into the main tunnel belowground. But all he did was sit there. For hours he just sat, and I sat, until I started to get restless. Of course, it was the moment when I left to use the bathroom that he did it. I came back to find the whole thing over. The little guy was back in his tunnel, but I could tell from the chamber that he'd excavated a side tunnel, drilling right across into the main burrow.

I started setting up five or six beetle farms at a time, all with mixtures of large and small males, and sure enough, I finally saw the sneaking firsthand. After sitting still for hours, the little male suddenly stirred, pushing into the side of the main tunnel and shooting down the shaft to the female. He could mate with the female and bolt right back out again in just a couple of minutes, while the guarding male blocked the entrance above, oblivious to the intruder.

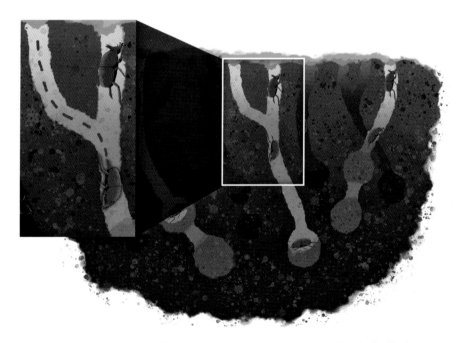

Small males can't win in a straight fight, so they sneak into tunnels on the sly. By digging side tunnels, small males can find and mate with the female while the guarding male blocks the entrance unaware.

When I told my professors about the side tunnels they challenged me, pointing out that these beetles were digging in skinny glass sandwiches, a *two-dimensional* universe. Where else were the little guys going to go? Of course they'd occasionally bump into the main tunnel in a beetle farm. The real question was whether they did the same thing in the wild. Armed with tubes of warm silicone caulking (like you'd use to seal around the edges of a bathtub), I squirted white goo into tunnels in the forest. Pieces of monkey dung aren't very big—maybe the size of a silver dollar—and it was not uncommon for there to be entrances to ten or twenty separate tunnels crammed into the soil beneath them. So I filled them all with silicone, then dug the whole thing up and carted it back to the lab where I could gently wash away the soil, revealing rubber casts of the tunnels.

Not only did side tunnels happen in the wild, they happened a lot. It was clear from the casts that sneaky males could hit four or five guarded tunnels with each of their horizontal shafts. Now I understood why big males periodically patrolled their tunnels, and I was beginning to understand why small males don't have horns. In this species, like many of the tunneling dung beetles, the largest males all grow a pair of long horns, but the smaller males do not. They don't even have intermediate horns. Instead, they look a lot like females. Fighting wasn't working, so these little guys switched to "plan B." While big males with long horns fought their fights, sneaky little males without horns wormed into tunnels on the sly!

Clearly, big weapons can be very expensive. So expensive, in fact, that the smallest males in my beetle species didn't even bother producing them, taking their chances instead as cheaters, worming into guarded tunnels on the sly. Surely the staggering cost helps explain why most animal species don't have big weapons; giant, awkward, fighting structures just aren't worth the price.

Another piece to my puzzle was falling into place. My mystery—explaining why species do or do not have big weapons—likely boiled down to understanding the delicate balance between benefits and costs. If in most species most of the time the benefits of big weapons are small, then costs should keep evolutionary increases in weapon size in check. Males that stumbled on a bigger weapon would do *worse*, not better, than their rivals since the benefits they gleaned from these structures wouldn't be enough to justify the cost.

Explaining big weapons meant focusing on the exceptions to this rule. Under what ecological conditions might the benefits of big weapons be so great that they outweighed the costs?

FIGHTERS AND SNEAKS

The dung beetles I studied had two types of males. Big males wielded a pair of long horns and used these weapons in battles for access to females. The biggest males were the most likely to win fights, and they were the ones who guarded tunnels. What if you're not the biggest male in the population? Sometimes the sausage of buried dung—the food your mom stashed for you to eat as you grew—wasn't very big. For these unlucky males the food ran out before they'd gotten very large. In principle, they could still grow horns, short ones, anyway, and they could always try to fight. But their chances of winning are poor. So these tiny males break the rules and cheat. Males without much food as they develop switch to a different path. They don't waste energy growing a horn that won't help them. Instead, they emerge from metamorphosis looking an awful lot like a little female. Sleek and small, their "weapon-free" shape helps them slip into the tunnels of other males.

PART 4

When Benefits
Outweigh Costs

JOURNAL ENTRY 2 *My First Trip to Panama*

Morning sun cuts through thick mist rising from the Chagres River, the water source for the Panama Canal, and steam lifts from the tropical forest nearby. It is unbearably humid, and biting flies nip at our ankles and the soles of our bare feet. We crouch in the canoe, trying to get comfortable as we follow our focal birds. I'm using binoculars, sweat already dripping down my arms as they steady my view, elbows planted on the hot aluminum rim of the boat. My dad sits behind me peering through a spotting telescope. Mounted on a tripod and perched rather precariously between us, the scope is trained on a male jacana, who just this morning hatched four chicks.

This was 1987; three years before I would begin working on beetles—before I was even aware that dung beetles on Barro Colorado Island existed. I had traveled to Panama with my dad. I was a sophomore in college and he a professor. He was setting up a research program studying jacanas, and I'd tagged along for a month to help out.

Each morning we drove to the edge of the river where an old Grumman canoe lay chained to a tree. After loading water, lunch, ponchos, clipboards, and binoculars, we'd paddle a mile upriver and cross the huge channel to the far side, where a number of floating mats of green sat in a wide eddy, as stationary as islands floating on the surface of a river can be. Here, he'd placed unique combinations of colored rings on the legs of all of the territorial birds—the ones able to hold on to the precious vegetative real estate—and we spent day after day spying on our avian actors as their lives unfolded on this patchwork of swirling, drifting stages.

Jacanas are bizarre birds, especially when it comes to their weapons. Black, slender bodies contrast starkly with yellow bills, long yellow wing spurs, and wrinkled, fleshy wattles—folded globs of feather-free skin that look like pieces of chewed, cherry-red bubble gum squished onto their foreheads. The female I'm watching has especially big spurs, one on each elbow, and she creeps about with delicate steps on very long legs. Her slender toes splay to a span of more than five inches per foot, and her gait makes me think of a circus stilt-walker.

This female, red-over-blue (she's named for the colored rings on her leg), is making the rounds of her territory, checking the nests of each of her four mates. Her territory is difficult to get to, and we have to watch at a distance from a canoe. Jacanas defend areas of floating vegetation on wide tropical rivers. Panamanians call them "Jesus" birds because they look like they walk on the water, and, in a sense, they do. They tiptoe across their floating mats, dispersing weight with each step over delicate toes, balancing atop the bobbing rosettes of water lettuce and hyacinth. Most predators can't reach jacanas out here, since they'd sink through the thin mat into the river. Crocodiles and caiman, however, swim under the mats and float up into the lettuce, snatching birds from below.

This morning, red-over-blue is fighting again, as she so often does. An unmarked female has darted in from the adjacent shoreline, hiding in the hyacinth leaves behind one of the males, but our territorial female spots her immediately and closes in. Now, face-to-face, the two birds size each other up. Crouching low, elbow spurs flared out to the sides, each sidesteps the other in a slow circle. Then red-over-blue pounces, leaping into the air and striking the intruder feet-first on her way down, slashing out with her wing spurs. Everything whirls into a blur as both birds leap at each other over and over, crashing together and jabbing as they flail onto the mat of floating lettuce, pop to their feet, and leap once more. And then suddenly the fight is over; the intruder flies away, and the thick air rings with raucous "ka-ka-ka-ka's" as our focal female proclaims victory to birds nearby.

Female jacanas are fighters, towering over the males. They are stronger than males, vastly more aggressive, and they have the larger weapons. Sharp yellow spurs jut forward like daggers from each elbow. Bigger females fare better in fierce battles and, as a rule, only dominant, top-condition females manage to hold a territory for long enough to breed.

The sky cracks with a boom and warm rain begins to pour down (it does this a lot in Panama). Torrents of water dump over us as we scramble to cover the scope and our notes with ponchos and plastic. The *birds hunker down to sit out the deluge. We hunker down too and wait, exposed and shivering as lightning crackles around our little metal boat. Ten minutes later the storm has passed and we, and the birds, are back at it. Three inches of water sloshes along the floor of our canoe, so we flip a plastic milk crate on its head and use it as a table to keep our gear clear. Red-over-blue is engaged in yet another fight— her fourth of the morning—and I check in with my dad. The male he's following shepherds his brand-new chicks as they wobble from plant to plant, all feeding on little insects squirming at the water surface around the lettuce.*

Ready to catch jacanas on the Chagres River. To mark the birds with colored ring bands, we first had to catch them, and this wasn't easy on floating islands of water lettuce. The plants in the canoe have been stapled to a floating board with a spring-loaded net, to try to trap a territorial female as she approaches a decoy.

Taking notes on the river while watching jacanas.

CHAPTER 12

Why Is It (Almost) Always Males?

In every way that matters for this book, jacanas are backwards. Females are more aggressive than males, they are larger than males, they fight more viciously and frequently than males, and females have larger weapons. Usually it's the other way around. In flies, beetles, mastodons, crabs, and caribou, males are armed, not females. Jacanas excepted, in every species with weapons confined to a single sex, males have those weapons. Why should just one sex have weapons? And why is it almost always the males?

One striking characteristic of the most gargantuan animal weapons is they are much bigger in males than they are in females. Females either don't produce the weapons at all or, if they do, the weapons they carry are tiny—nothing outlandish or out of proportion, or awkward in any way. This is because females put their energy into other things. In all of these animals, females spend a great deal of time feeding and protecting their offspring. They pack eggs with nutrients like proteins and fats and sugars; they protect babies as they grow, often carrying them inside their bodies (many flies and cockroaches do this too, not just mammals); and sometimes they protect them from harm after they hatch or are born. Although the details differ from species to species—caribou, for example, hold fetuses in their womb, while crabs and crickets guard eggs in burrows underground—females in all of these species put considerable effort into their young.

When females like these reproduce, it takes them a long time, and, as a result, they can't produce babies very often. They are only receptive to mating every once in a while. Males in these same species hardly invest in the babies at all, and they are free to breed again much sooner. In fact, in most of these animals, the males leave right away after mating, turning their efforts toward seeking new females and new opportunities to breed.

There's a problem here—a glaring one—and it's all about numbers. If you walked into a natural population of one of these animal species and counted how many males and how many females were ready to breed *right now*—at this very moment—you'd find a big difference. Just about all the males would be ready, but many of the females would not. Females taking care of young—nursing, for example, or pregnant—couldn't make new babies at that moment even if they wanted to. Their bodies aren't ready. Only a few of the females, the ones who just finished raising a batch of young, would be physically able to reproduce at that moment in time.

In animals like this there tend to be a lot more males cruising around looking for females than there are females looking for males. Because reproductively ready females are in very short supply (female elephants, for example, are only receptive to males for five days out of every four years), there aren't enough to go around. There are way too many males, and the result is competition—often, very intense competition.

Surpluses of reproductively ready males definitely don't occur in all animals, and there are even species where it works the other way

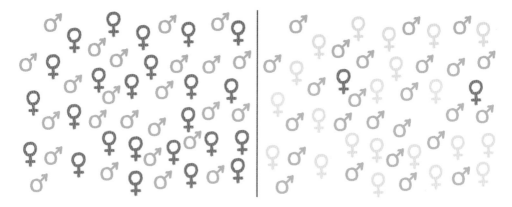

Even though a population may have roughly equal numbers of males and females (that is, a "head count" would yield about the same number of each [left]), this can be misleading. The more appropriate question to ask is "How many males and females are ready to reproduce *right now*?" In species like caribou, elk, and dung beetles, a survey of who's available for breeding would show that almost all the males are ready to breed, but most of the females are not. Many females could not breed right then because they are either pregnant or taking care of young, and their bodies are not capable of making new babies (faded symbols in the figure to the right). When this happens, males face intense competition with rival males for access to the small number of available females.

Elephant moms can breed only five days every four years.

around (in pipefish, sea spiders, and some shorebirds like jacanas, for example, an abundance of females competes for chances to mate with a small number of available males). But excesses of males are universal in the species with the biggest weapons. The intense battles that result when too many males fight for not enough females favor males with traits that aid them in these brawls. Traits like weapons.

When competition is fierce enough, the benefits of big weapons can outweigh the costs. Occasionally, when the conditions are just right, bigger weapons perform better than smaller weapons. Males with the biggest weapons win—they hold the best territories, or guard the largest groups of females. These males, the ones brandishing the most outlandish weapons, prevail.

Because receptive females are in very short supply, elephant bulls face intense competition for opportunities to breed.

CHAPTER 13

Many Weapons, One Story

Beetle horns are just one example of the wealth of outlandish and spectacular animal weapons. Long horns rise from the skulls of dozens of antelope species, like the twisting spires of kudu; the graceful, curving arcs of ibex and sable; the coiled horns of waterbuck and impala; or the sideways curls of bighorn sheep, to name just a few. Then there are the antlers—branched bone weapons gracing the heads of deer, elk, moose, and caribou—and the tusks of walruses and narwhals.

Even some insects have "tusks" of a sort—a reclusive genus of African wasps and a New Zealand cricket—though they are made of exoskeleton (chitin) rather than ivory, and some New Guinean flies have "antlers." Males of one of these species have broad, flat antlers ringed with points that reach out to the sides of their heads, making these flies look like miniature moose.

Other insects, most notably beetles but also a number of bugs, have grossly exaggerated legs that function as weapons. Thick,

Caribou bull with huge antlers.

Narwhal tusks.

bulging hind legs in "frog-legged" leaf beetles are so grotesquely big that the males waddle as they walk, and the chopstick-length front legs of another beetle, the harlequin beetle, must be pulled up and folded out of the way when males aren't fighting, causing the biggest males to be awkward and gangly.

Walrus tusks.

In fact, a survey of animal diversity reveals crazy-big weapons in thousands of species, ranging from antelope, sheep, deer, and lizards, to crabs, shrimp, bees, wasps, beetles, bugs, daddy longlegs, and flies. What's remarkable about these weapons, however, is that they all share one thing in common. Despite being carried by an incredible diversity of animals lurking in habitats as different as ocean floors, rain forests, alpine tundra, and desert, all of these weapons serve the same purpose. Their stories are the same story, and it's all about competition: battles between rival males over females.

Moose fly with "antlers."

Frog-legged leaf beetle with huge hind leg weapons.

Males competing for females is nothing new, and all of this was known before I started my project. Darwin actually came up with the idea way back in 1871, and many researchers had explored the theory from there. But male competition was not the whole story. It couldn't be, because many thousands of animal species had intense male competition *but no weapons*, or, at least, not ridiculously large ones. Males in these species competed in other ways—peacocks competed to wave the brightest displays, and birds and frogs competed to sing with the loudest or most complex or attractive songs. Still other species actually fought battles, but these battles did not include bulky weapons (ball-rolling dung beetles, for example). Clearly, competition could take many forms, and only occasionally did it lead to the evolution of big weapons.

WHY KNIGHTS IN SHINING ARMOR WERE LIKE ELEPHANTS

During the height of the Middle Ages (1300–1500), men fought battles for access to women just as bull elephants do for their mates. Here, too, intense competition led rapidly to extreme weapons.

At this time, wealth was tied up in the hands of local lords and noble families who clung tenaciously to their holdings. In an effort to keep their riches consolidated, noble families adopted strict rules of inheritance. Entire estates had to be passed intact to just one child, generally the eldest son. This avoided the problem of dividing lands, splitting holdings into smaller and smaller parcels each generation; it kept power firmly consolidated—at least for the eldest son.

All of the other sons in these families—and often there were a lot— were left with no lands and no future. Without an estate to their name, these men were not seen as good matches for noble daughters of other estates. In fact, the only way a younger son could marry was if he succeeded in winning the favors of an heiress—a woman who already had an estate of her own. Occasionally, all of the male heirs to a family died, and when this happened the estate passed to a daughter. Just as in elephants, where females only became receptive to breeding for five days out of every four years, noble heiresses were exceedingly rare. But such an heiress had the power to pick whomever she wished for a husband.

"Knights-errant"—literally, the "wandering knights"—spent decades learning to fight. Starting as early as age seven, these surplus sons of noble families apprenticed with experienced tutors. Training constantly,

Knights battling in a tournament. During the Middle Ages, suits of armor were exorbitantly expensive. Only the wealthiest knights could afford them, and they'd become so bulky and heavy that if a knight fell onto his back he was as helpless as an overturned turtle.

they shadowed elder warriors into battle, practicing tactics and combat. As they came of age, they began to seek status and rank. Battles allowed them to prove their valor, but tournaments—ritualized contests of skill and strength—gave them chances to show off in front of the women.

Tournaments were magnificent spectacles. Noble women sat ringside in grandstands while rival knights clashed with swords or jousting lances. The knights themselves glistened in the sun, resplendent in spectacular suits of expensive armor, engraved meticulously with intricate artistic patterns and covered with vivid tunics of blazing color. Knights even wore elaborate feather plumes on the tops of their helmets.

Knights showed off in every way they possibly could, like strutting peacocks bedazzled in color. But the heart of the tournament was always the fight. Rival knights slashed and stabbed at each other in front of the women. Most knights fought hundreds of battles without ever winning the hand of an heiress. Those very few who did—the absolute best of the best—only won their status (and their wives) after forty or more years of continuous battle. The same age, incidentally, as successful bull elephants.

FIGHTING FEMALES

Although it is very rare, there are a few species of animals where females do the fighting. One mentioned in Journal Entry 2, on page 74—the jacana—even lives in Panama. Barro Colorado Island sits in the middle of a huge lake called Gatun Lake, and this lake is filled with water flowing in from the Chagres River. If you paddle a canoe about five miles or so up the Chagres, you'll find yourself surrounded by jacanas.

Jacanas are unusual because males raise the young. Females defend big territories on the floating mats, and the biggest territories house three or four males. Each male makes a nest in a different part of her territory, tucked into a sheltered nook of the vegetation, and the female visits the males in turn and lays eggs into each of the nests. The males then sit on the eggs to incubate them, and, once the eggs hatch, the dads stay with the chicks, shepherding them around as they wobble unsteadily on the

Jacana chick with long toes, ideal for walking on floating islands of water lettuce.

Jacana males are smaller than females, and the males do all the work of parenting. Here a female towers over a male.

floating lettuce. He guards them as they learn to walk and feed, and he guards them as they grow. He'll stay with them until they're ready to fly off on their own, a period of up to three months.

All the while, the female stays by herself, flying back and forth across her territory, warding off intruder females. She's not involved with raising the chicks at all. In jacanas, males invest more time raising the young than females do. It takes them longer to recycle in between batches of babies. A female can lay a clutch of eggs into one male's nest and, three weeks later, she's ready to lay a new batch into the next nest. Males, on the other hand, are committed to chicks for eleven weeks. Now, we can ask the same question we did for caribou, elephants, and beetles: "How many males and females are ready to reproduce *right now*?" This time, however, we get the opposite answer. There are more *females* ready to breed than *males*. In jacanas, females must compete with rival females for access to a small number of reproductively available males—not the other way around.

Jacana females fight fierce battles for their territories, and for the males whose nests are tucked away in them. Female jacanas are bigger than males, they are more aggressive than males, and they have the bigger weapons. Jacanas are a beautiful exception that "proves the rule." Most of the time, however, big weapons are borne by the males.

Because available males are in very short supply, female jacanas fight battles with rival females for access to these males. Note the yellow spurs on this dominant female.

CHAPTER 14

Unanswered Questions

By the end of my time in the rain forest I'd learned a lot about beetle horns, as well as animal weapons in general. I'd learned that males fight vicious battles with rival males for opportunities to breed with females, and that in some species, such as my dung beetles, males use big weapons in these battles. Beetle horns clearly helped males win fights, and males with the longest horns were the most likely to win ownership of tunnels containing females.

I'd shown that beetle horns are expensive, stunting the growth of eyes, and I'd also shown that only the best-conditioned males could afford to pay this price. For example, by adding or removing dung from the little sausages made by females, I changed the amount of food available to each larva. Some grubs now had lots of food; others had only a little. Males with access to the most food emerged as adults with the largest body sizes, and it was these males—the best-fed, biggest males—who produced the largest weapons.

Along the way I'd fallen in love with the rain forest. Forty miles of

Fairchild

Lab Buildings

Nemesia

Barbour

Schneirla

Van Tyne

Barro Colorado Island has
more than 40 miles of trails.

trails sprawled out from the field station like spokes from a wheel, snaking along twisted ridges, cutting through streambeds and ravines, and extending to the tips of each of the forested tentacles of the four-thousand-acre island. Now, after more than six hundred hikes into the forest, I knew the terrain like the back of my hand. The

Another tunneling dung beetle
species with horns.

major trails were named for early biologists, and I could picture the forest they passed through in my head. There was "Schneirla," for example, jutting like an artery straight up to the main plateau in the center of the island. "Fairchild" wrapped north and then east into dry, thin forest, while "Barbour" cut southeast, through dense stands of extremely tall trees. There, the forest was dark and damp, clinging to steep sides of muddy ravines. "Van Tyne" circled around the biggest tree I'd ever seen, a massive Ceiba with support buttresses the size of a barn, and a canopy towering two hundred feet above the forest floor.

My favorite trail was "Nemesia." Little traveled, this one wound into a hilly part of the island coursing with streams and waterfalls. If you cut left at the third stream and worked off-trail through the tangle for

Resting in the waterfall at my secret spot, off the Nemesia trail.

Violaceous trogon.

A tamandua (anteater) searches for food.

about half a mile, you'd emerge into a magical place. The forest peeled back into a little clearing surrounding a sparkling pool, resting at the bottom of a gentle, sloping waterfall. As far as I could tell I was the only person who knew of this place, and I'd sit in the cool stream, relaxing back onto the sloping cascade, and let water rush over and around me as I listened to parrots overhead.

I knew the sweaty stink of wild pigs, and the distant crashes and branch-rattles of each of the different types of monkey: white-faced capuchin, spider, and howler. I knew the soft flutter of wingbeats characteristic to motmots and trogons, my favorite birds of the dark understory. Most of all, I thought I finally understood my beetles.

But I had that one lingering problem I still couldn't solve. One frustrating piece to the puzzle remained missing. Clearly, fierce competition among rival males was part of the story—there was no question that this was the backdrop for the horns in my beetles, just as it was in so many other species with big weapons. But competition wasn't enough. It was *necessary*, I now realized, but not sufficient, because lots of very closely related species did not invest in big weapons.

Why would big weapons arise in some of these beetles but not others?

* * *

Butterflies often perched in the sun spots of the forest understory, illuminating their shiny wings.

In Ecuador, I'd set out to study rhinoceros beetles with and without horns, in the hopes that I'd be able to discover what was different. I wanted to identify that special ingredient that tipped the balance between benefits and costs, helping explain why particular species invested in big weapons. Now, at the end of my time in Panama, I was back where I'd started, confronted with the simple fact that sitting right beside my beetles *with* horns were lots of very similar species that lacked horns. In order to understand why some species have big weapons, I was going to have to explain why so many other species didn't.

This fact stared me in the face each day as I hiked into the forest to find beetles, because ball-rolling species do not have horns. Ball-rolling beetles battled too. Their resources—little balls of dung—were small and defensible, just like a tunnel, and, in principle, males should have been able to guard them. Their females invested substantial time and effort into the provisioning of young, like the tunneling species. And, as a result, their populations contained an overabundance of eager males fighting for chances to breed. Male ball-rolling beetles competed just like the tunnelers did. In fact, everything about these beetles was similar to the tunnelers. They lived in the same forest during the same seasons. They were active at the same times of day, and they colonized the exact same pieces of dung.

So why didn't ball-rolling beetles have big weapons?

This was no easy question to answer, and by the time I completed my studies in 1994, I still had no solution. I moved on to apprentice in another lab with a biologist at Duke University who studied the ways insects develop. My research questions shifted from "Why do only some species have horns?" to "How do beetles make their horns?" and "Why do only the biggest, best-conditioned males grow the longest horns?" Years passed, and I moved yet again, this time to take a position as a professor at the University of Montana. It wasn't until I traveled to Africa almost ten years later that my original mystery started haunting me once again.

I still couldn't figure out why ball-rolling beetles never had horns. For that mystery, I would have to travel to the heart of dung beetle diversity, Africa.

CHAPTER 15

Serengeti National Park

Our truck lurched to a stop, rocking slightly, dust from the dry roadbed billowing up in a cloud. Fifteen of us sat packed in an open-sided, off-road capable safari "minivan." I was one of three University of Montana professors teaching a field course on the ecology of East Africa. Nine graduate students filled out the ranks, along with three Tanzanian guides.

The night before, we'd gotten our first taste of the dangers of being "in the bush." After a hearty camp dinner prepared by our guides, we'd settled into our tents and tried to fall asleep. This was harder than it might seem, given the general excitement of being in Africa and the cacophony of wild sounds—hoots and guffaws of hyenas, honking squeaks of zebra, and, most disconcerting of all, the crackling rustle of huge unknown animals snapping branches as they pushed through the brush in the dark. Some of us drifted off to sleep faster than others, but we all woke with a start when lions entered the camp.

Sunset at our Tanzania camp.

In they came, circling around our tents in the moonlight, shadows looming large on paper-thin nylon fabric walls. One of them growled softly as she sniffed the zipper at the front of my tent, her throaty purr sending a panicked shiver down my spine. She was *right outside*—not two feet from my face! Nobody dared step out of their tent until the guards sounded the "all clear" the next morning.

Now, bouncing along rutted dirt tracks in the savanna, searching for game, we were hyper-aware of danger lurking unseen in the surrounding scrub. Being eaten was on all of our minds because I'd added a twist to the routine of this year's class. I had permits allowing us to collect dung beetles inside the park.

Africa is the epicenter of dung beetle diversity, a land teeming with billions of beetles. But to find them we had to get out of the truck—something that is strictly forbidden here, and for very good reason. Getting out of the car in this national park is a good way to get killed. The most likely villains are actually not lions, although many thousand live in the park. Statistically, the most dangerous animal is the Cape buffalo. Massive, irritable, and practically blind, their reaction to most things is simply to charge. Hippos, crocodiles, and irate elephants could kill you too, as well as cheetahs, hyenas, and leopards. Basically, when you're in a park like the Serengeti, it's best to stay in the car.

Cape buffalo, the number one reason *not* to get out of our vehicle.

But we needed beetles, so our guides laid down the law. We could venture out of the vehicle only when they were ready, meaning after one of them was in position on the van roof and the other two were set up on each side as spotters. Then, and only then, could we dash into the field beside the road—not getting too close to any bushes and remaining in constant line-of-sight view of the spotters. We had to work fast—very fast—and we had to be ready to jump back into the van in an instant if they sounded the alarm.

On went the surgical gloves. Everybody grabbed a bucket or jar to hold beetles, I picked up a shovel, and we jumped from the truck. Our target was a pile of zebra dung in the grass, and in a flash we flipped it into a wide Tupperware bin, pulling apart the moist fragments and plucking dozens of shiny metallic beetles from the bottom of the bin as they scrabbled across the slippery surface. I dug a shovelful of tunnel-riddled soil from beneath where the dung had been, tipping it into another bin, and began sifting through the dirt

Africa had millions of dung beetles and ten times as many species as Panama. But here, too, ball rollers never had horns, while tunnelers often did.

with my fingers, extracting beetles. In no time we'd collected several hundred dung beetles—a good catch. But this was high-stress and potentially high-risk beetle collecting. We needed a better strategy.

We got one later that day in the form of a massive pile of elephant dung. A family of elephants had blocked our path, staring us down from the middle of the track. We'd waited, tensely watching and snapping photos as they first inspected our vehicle and then ambled past us into the surrounding scrub (traffic stops for elephants here, not the other way around). Now, steaming in a pothole beside our van, sat the largest pile of dung any of us had ever seen. Here was our new strategy: This dung was fresh enough that we could bring it

Hunting for beetles in Africa was an adventure! We had to have a guard perched on the roof of the car behind us, watching out for leopards, lions, Cape buffalo, or angry elephants. We gathered beetles as fast as we could, rushing back to the car whenever something dangerous came too close.

back to camp and let the beetles come to us. I scooped it into a five-gallon plastic bucket and sealed the lid tight. That evening, after a long and dusty day bird-watching and mammal-spotting, I placed the dung onto moist soil away from our tents and sat back with a ring of students wearing headlamps to see what would happen next.

Never in twenty years of traveling the world in search of beetles have I witnessed an abundance of insects like I did that night. In Panama there had been roughly twenty different beetle species attracted to monkey dung. Here there were more than a hundred species all converging on one single pile of elephant dung. When they first arrived I tried to catch them, count them, and place each in a separate glass vial, but soon they came too fast. Even with five helpers beside me all attempting to catch and record these animals, we couldn't keep up. Beetles began to spin into our headlamps and plonk onto

The best source of dung was the elephant, but finding fresh elephant dung had its own challenges, like this angry bull!

clipboards and into our laps, and like rain they fell from the sky. They began dropping by dozens at once. Beetles were tumbling into our hair and down the backs of our necks, and the mass of beetles that landed on my notepad was so thick I had to sweep them aside to write. It was as if somebody poured beetles from a bucket over our heads and onto the dung. Our best (and admittedly rough) estimate was that more than *one hundred thousand* beetles converged on that single pile of dung that night.

Tourists may flock to the Serengeti to see lions or elephants or gazelles with twisted horns, but it is the tiny dung beetle who displays the most dazzling weapons here. Just in that one sample, we observed all sorts of impressive weapons. But there were just as many species with *no weapons at all.* Here, once more, was my mystery, back after all these years to haunt me: same season, same habitat, even the same pile of dung, yet only the tunneling species invested in large weapons.

What was so special about fighting inside of a tunnel?

CHAPTER 16

The Answer at Last, in an Unlikely Place

Observing the "haves" and "have-nots" of Tanzanian dung beetles rekindled my quest in a flash. The pattern in Africa was *exactly the same* as in Panama! Only the tunnelers had horns. Like a hound racing to follow a scent, I was now back "on-mission," and determined to solve my original mystery.

I began poring through the academic literature in earnest, tracking down every paper I could find on big weapons—all weapons, any weapons, and the bigger the better. I filled file cabinets with papers on fossils—triceratops and trilobites and Irish elk—and papers on frog fangs, cricket tusks, fly antlers, and crab claws. Species after species, I stacked up what I could find, assembling morsels of biology and scribbling them on flash cards spread out in piles across my desk and tables.

It was exciting and encouraging that so many different types of animal weapons all worked the same way—their stories were essentially the same story. But nobody had found the missing piece to my puzzle. The crucial clue was utterly absent from the biological literature, not even on the "radar screen" of most of the scientists studying animal weapons. So I cast a wider net and began looking at military weapons too. Manufactured weapons like guns and tanks and ships also evolve, it turns out, and just as with animals, they sometimes get sucked into an arms race, surging forward to bigger and bigger sizes.

In the end it was the military scholars, not biologists, who held my final clue. I found the answer to my mystery in dusty books about military battles—hand-to-hand brawls of Greek and Roman soldiers, epic clashes of ancient oared galleys, the combat tactics of tanks and airplanes, and even the wars that arise between nations.

Here were writings of a different sort of researcher—untrained in biology and largely uninterested in animal behavior. Yet these historians studied arms races too, and many had sought to explain the exact same question as I did. When and why do weapons get big?

Two thousand five hundred years ago, warships powered by rows of long oars, called galleys, grew so massive—the biggest was 420 feet long and rowed by four thousand men—they became clumsy and unmanageable. Six hundred years ago, suits of plate armor had become so bulky and heavy that a knight who fell off his horse was as helpless as an overturned turtle—unable even to stand up by himself. By the beginning of the nineteenth century, sailing warships bristling with cannons were so large that building a single ship required wood from eleven thousand oak trees. Similar excesses occurred with steam-powered warships (called "ironclads"), with tanks, and with nuclear warheads, missiles, and aircraft carriers (a single US Navy *Nimitz*-class aircraft carrier and its associated "strike group"—the gaggle of ships that always surrounds it—costs more than $20 billion to produce).

Once I began to explore this literature I stepped into a world rich with unbelievable weapons and full of extremes. Over and over throughout our past, simple changes in technology plunged these

Human weapons get caught up in arms races too, leading to weapons just as extravagant as in animals. In the ancient Mediterranean, oared warships grew so large they became unwieldy. The largest ship ever recorded from antiquity, called "Ptolemy's forty" was 420 feet long and was rowed by four thousand men.

"First-rate" ships of the line, the most extravagant and expensive warships in their day, cost a fortune to build. The wooden hull of one of these ships took all the timber from eleven thousand oak trees.

weapons into an arms race. From that point forward, bigger was better—a lot better—and nations raced to improve their weapons by frantically equaling and then surpassing the weapons of their rivals.

Both sides got sucked into these races, as each leapfrogged past the other in back-and-forth cycles that led to bigger, faster, or otherwise better weapons.

Just as in animals, these military arms races surged forward until they peaked with weapons of absurd sizes and costs, at which point the process often collapsed. The more I read, the more I realized that these cycles were *exactly the same*. It didn't matter if I was talking about beetles or battleships, crabs or the Cold War; arms races were arms races, period.

The specific piece to my puzzle—the ingredient for sparking an arms race that I'd been missing all these years—was *duels*. Opponents had to square off one-on-one, in face-to-face matchups of fighting ability and strength.

The first person to figure out the special significance of duels actually tackled this problem during the First World War (1914–1918). He was a strange and brilliant automobile engineer named Frederick Lanchester. Lanchester figured out that one simple change in behavior made all the difference. When opponents confront each other in scrambles, chaotic clashes of ships or soldiers, then investing in expensive weapons is a mistake. The outcome of scrambles is unpredictable, so the reward for investing in big weapons is small. Why pay the steep price of an extreme weapon if it might not even help you in a fight?

Another way to think about this is strength in numbers: When lots of rivals all attack at the same time, then they can overwhelm even the biggest weapons. In that situation, having big weapons is a waste. On the other hand, when opponents face each other one at a time, the fights are much more consistent; the outcome is repeatable. In these fights, the opponent with the best weapons almost always wins. In duels, because the winner is usually the one with the most advanced weapons, investing in big weapons *is* worth the price.

When Lanchester worked through this logic, he compared battles

In ancient battles soldiers fought each other face-to-face—as each man attacked the man across from him in the line.

in the ancient world—close-range combat where a soldier fought the man across from him using a sword and shield—with more recent battles where soldiers lined up in a row and fired rifles simultaneously. If an army had to choose how to spend its resources, opting either to invest in expensive training and state-of-the-art rifles for its existing troops, or to invest in hiring more troops, then the answer depended on the type of battle. In the modern world, he proposed, where soldiers no longer fought in duels, investing in expensive weapons was a mistake. Just hire more troops, because in these fights the army with the most soldiers was likely to win.

Although Lanchester himself never saw the link between his logic and arms races, later scholars did. Lanchester was interested in when you *shouldn't* invest in big weapons. But flip his logic around, and you also have an answer for the question of when you *should*. Duels, Lanchester's logic suggested, could create situations where bigger weapons performed better than smaller ones, starting an arms race. And duels could arise between lots of things—not just soldiers on a line of battle. Warships had to confront rival warships, and these encounters could play out as either scrambles or duels. Fighter air-

Frederick Lanchester explored the costs and benefits of governments investing in armies. He pointed out that in ancient battles troops tended to fight one-on-one with the man across from them. Because they marched into battle shoulder to shoulder in lines, there was no room for soldiers to gang up on each other, and fights played out in a series of successive duels. In these fights, it often pays to invest in extensive training and state-of-the-art weapons.

Lanchester noted that battles fought after the invention of gunpowder did not occur as duels. Now troops could all concentrate their fire. By ganging up and firing simultaneously, armies with more soldiers overpowered rival forces with fewer soldiers. In fights where soldiers gang up on opponents, it rarely pays to invest in expensive weapons, because adding more soldiers is always the better way to win.

Soldiers in the First World War concentrating their fire.

craft faced off against fighter aircraft, and tanks against rival tanks. Even nations challenging other nations could do so in the context of a scramble or a duel.

Here was a simple change in behavior, from a scramble to a duel, that military scholars had already recognized could help explain why some weapons—guns, ships, and tanks, for example—got really big while others did not. But nobody had ever thought about this in animals. If Lanchester's logic worked for military weapons, I wondered, why couldn't it work for animal weapons too?

CHIVALRY AND DUELS

One of the oldest examples of writing to survive to the present day is a poem penned by a Greek named Homer. The *Iliad*, written in a rhythmic cadence designed to be read aloud, had been passed from storyteller to storyteller for hundreds of years before it ever was inked onto parchment. It tells a grand tale of a heroic fighter, a warrior in the purest sense of the term. His name was Achilles.

Achilles Slays Hector, painted in 1630–32 by Peter Paul Rubens, depicts the classic duel between heroes in Homer's *Iliad.*

In the midst of a long, winding adventure, this poem explores what it means to be a hero. It describes honor and bravery, and fierce combat. It also describes *duels.* Rivals sized each other up beforehand, and conflict progressed through a ritualized sequence of steps. First, each rode onto the field of battle in a horse-drawn chariot. Then, stepping off, each warrior explained who he was to the other fighter, listing the foes he'd vanquished already to get there. Then they stood a fixed distance apart and hurled spears. Next, provided the spears missed, which they typically did, the fighters moved closer and lunged with a different type of spear. Finally, if neither had backed down, the battle culminated with a close-quarter, hand-to-hand brawl where swords, shields, and skill ruled the day.

Homeric duels epitomized honorable battle for thousands of years, throughout the Classical era of ancient Greece (circa 500–300 BCE) and the Roman Empire (circa 27 BCE–1453 CE). They formed the basis for chivalry during the Middle Ages (circa 500–1500), and many aspects of this view of honor in battle persist to this day. This is what Lanchester envisioned when he described ancient warfare as duels, and this is the sort of battle where expensive weapons mattered a lot. Ritualized, repeatable, and fair. When rivals faced off toe-to-toe in a duel, the better fighter—and this often meant the one with the better weapons—won.

CHAPTER 17

The Final Piece of My Puzzle

I realized with a thrill as I pored through my note cards, scribbles, and journals that the same crucial ingredient—duels—*did* apply to animal weapons too. In dung beetles, for example, ball rollers fight aboveground in pile-on frays that are clearly scrambles. Three, four, or even more males will all jump into the battle at once, resulting in a tangle of writhing beetles clambering for possession of the ball of dung. These fights were exactly like the modern battles Lanchester described—chaotic and unpredictable. Males with big weapons might *not* win these fights if they got overwhelmed by multiple attackers. If we applied Lanchester's logic to ball-rolling dung beetles, then we'd predict that big weapons are not worth the price. Without the consistency or predictability of a duel, investing in big weapons would be an expensive mistake.

Tunneling beetles, on the other hand, always fought in duels for the simple reason that their battles took place underground and there was never enough room for more than two beetles to fight at a time.

Tunnels are *tubes,* confined spaces with a single opening at one end. How else could a beetle attack? He can't charge in from the side or behind, because the only way to confront a guarding male is to enter into the tube. It also is impossible for multiple males to attack all at once—they wouldn't fit inside the tunnel! Because fights unfolded inside the confines of a narrow tube, tunneling dung beetles always fought in one-on-one duels. And, as I'd shown already with my own experiments, in these fights males with the biggest weapons won.

Lanchester's logic worked. For dung beetles, big weapons are advantageous in species that fight inside tunnels, but not in species that scramble aboveground. What was so special about tunnels? *Duels.* Tunnels caused fights to take place as a series of one-on-one duels, rather than chaotic scrambles. The missing ingredient for dung beetle arms races was the duel.

PART 5

Following the Logic: Animal and Military Weapons Are the Same

CHAPTER 18

Triggering an Arms Race

One simple change in behavior—a shift in the way opponents faced each other in battle—can be enough to launch an arms race. In the military, shifts from scrambles to duels almost always resulted from new technologies. When ancient shipbuilders figured out how to add battering rams to the fronts of ships, oared galleys stopped being mere vessels of transport, hauling troops from place to place; now they could be warships. A galley with a battering ram could smash into a rival ship and sink it, provided it was fast enough. But it could only smash into one ship at a time—so these close-range clashes always took place as duels. One little change in technology—the addition of a battering ram—sparked an arms race, and from that point forward, galley sizes surged as navies raced to produce bigger and faster warships.

Faster in that age meant adding more rowers, so ships started to get longer and longer, until they buckled. Then shipbuilders started stacking rowers on top of one another on little shelves. One row of oars became two; two became three. Soon they were packing two or three men side by side at each oar, and "threes" became "fours" and then "fives." Soon there were "eights" and "nines," "elevens" and "thirteens." Ships got bigger and bigger until the race climaxed with a monstrosity called "Ptolemy's forty." After a thousand years with no change in ship design at all, a new technology altered the way ships confronted each other in battle, aligning them into close-range duels. From that point forward the race was on. In just three hundred years warships surged from penteconters rowed by fifty men, to massive, double-hulled behemoths powered by four thousand.

Oared galleys with battering rams fought rival ships at close range, in one-on-one duels, and this sparked an arms race in ship size.

A thousand years later the same thing happened all over again, only this time it was closeable gunports that did it, not battering rams. By this point, ships were powered by wind rather than oars, and sailing ships (called galleons) didn't make very good warships because their battering rams got stuck. Sailing ships couldn't back up after a strike, and the rigging on their masts tended to get tangled when ships smashed into each other. So battering rams had been removed and sailing ships switched back to being simple vehicles of transport, carrying cargo across the globe.

People tried mounting cannons on the decks of sailing galleons, but cannons were heavy and this much weight up high made the ships tippy. Closeable gunports—wooden hatches that could be opened in battle and latched tightly shut during a storm—changed all that. Hatches meant cannons could be mounted along the sides of ships, down low near the waterline. Weight down low made the ships *more* stable, not less, and suddenly everybody began mounting cannons along the sides of their ships.

Cannons were not accurate even under the best of conditions. On rocking ships in churning seas they were downright sloppy. The only way to actually hit an opponent was to sail right up beside them and

Sailing galleons also fought rivals in one-on-one duels because they could only fire their broadside at very close range. Duels sparked an arms race in the sizes of these ships too.

turn, unleashing a "broadside" at very close range. *Voilà!* In the technological blink of an eye sailing ships switched back to functioning as warships—weapons—and the fights they fought had to occur up close, in one-on-one duels. From that point forward ship sizes surged as builders added more and bigger cannons to larger and larger hulls. One row of cannons became two, two became three; six-pounders gave way to seven-pounders, then eight-pounders, and soon cannonball sizes climbed all the way to thirty-two and thirty-six pounds. More cannons, bigger cannons, the race was on.

The same thing happened when designers figured out how to mount machine guns onto the noses of the first aircraft. Overnight, planes switched their behavior from being battlefield spotters primarily used for intelligence gathering, to fighter planes embroiled

Adding machine guns to the noses of early aircraft led to another type of duel, aerial dogfighting. Here, also, duels sparked an arms race. This time, it favored faster and more maneuverable fighter planes.

in close-range dogfights. Over and over throughout history, simple changes in technology altered the way that soldiers or vehicles confronted each other in battle, and when this change meant that scrambles turned into one-on-one duels, it often started an arms race.

Jousting tournaments sparked an arms race in the weapons and armor of medieval knights. In every case, the trigger of the arms race was *duels*.

HOW CAN RIFLES OR BATTLESHIPS "EVOLVE"?

When elk antlers evolve, they do so because some individuals produce more offspring than others. Antlers are copied through reproduction, and winners in the battle for breeding make more copies of their antler type than losers do. Antlers evolve as the elk evolve—the two processes are inextricably linked, since the mechanism of replication of the weapons is the same as the mechanism of replication of the elk.

This is not true for our weapons. Manufactured weapons aren't parts of the body like tusks or horns. Their forms change over time in much the same way as animal weapons, but this change is not tied to evolution of humans. Particular weapon types can become more or less common independent of what happens to the people who use or carry them.

For example, consider the assault rifle. Instructions for building a rifle are transmitted through documents and computers (rather than DNA), but the result is faithful copying of the design from rifle to rifle. Rifles coming off an AK-47 assembly line are all AK-47s and not M16s or StG-44s. Yet, through accident or design, engineers are constantly adjusting rifle design, probing possibilities, and testing variations on the theme. Most of these experiments fail, but every now and then, new design features work and are rapidly incorporated into subsequent models. Most important of all, the realities of markets and battlefields act like agents of selection, discarding assault rifles that are too expensive to produce, that jam or misfire, or that are more cumbersome or awkward than other available alternatives. The conditions of warfare shape the evolution of assault rifles in much the same way that natural agents of selection, such as battles between rival males, shape the evolution of elk antlers.

As long as we focus on the *weapons*—antlers or rifles—and not the animals or humans using them, comparison of their respective evolutionary paths is helpful. What matters for the success or failure of a specific type of rifle is how well it performs relative to other rifle models in existence at the same time. The same can be said for ships, castles, and catapults. Designs that work are copied and spread; those that fail are abandoned. And, when the conditions are just right, these weapons can get swept up in arms races, surging forward to bigger and bigger sizes, deadlier, faster, and vastly more expensive, until the race climaxes with weapons of outlandish proportion and cost.

CHAPTER 19

Crickets, Crabs, Chameleons, and Caribou

Once I knew what to look for, I realized that the same simple change in behavior—a shift from scrambles to duels—explained arms races in lots of animal species. Some animals fight in frenzied acrobatic midair snarls. Others, like horseshoe crabs and ball-rolling dung beetles, pile onto rivals in chaotic scrambles. Big weapons don't help in these fights. They're not worth the price, either because the outcome is too unpredictable—too heavily influenced by chance—for investment in weapons to be worthwhile or because speed or agility matter more than bulk or strength. Big weapons slow you down. They get in the way, and fighting males that whirl around in the air would actually fare worse if they wielded big weapons.

Duels, on the other hand, are different. The outcome of duels is much more consistent and predictable. One-on-one fights very often stabilize into matched contests of size and strength. Males lock weapons and push or twist, straining against each other until one of the males yields. In these fights weapons matter a lot, and the bigger, stronger male—the male with the largest weapons—wins.

In dung beetles, the shift from scrambles to duels revolved around tunnels. When beetles began to fight inside tunnels their battles automatically became duels. Tunnels forced fights to play out one-on-one because only one rival could fit into the tunnel at a time. Suddenly, males with the biggest weapons began to win, and from that point forward populations evolved bigger and bigger horns.

It turns out tunnels trigger arms races in lots of animal species. Like battering rams, they tip the balance in favor of big weapons. Shrimp and crabs that fight over burrows often have huge claws. Wasps with long "tusks" fight over burrows, as do tusked wetas (a New Zealand relative of crickets) and big-headed male bees. There are even fanged frogs that fight over burrows, and there was a giant horned rodent, now extinct, that fought over burrows. In species after species, the constrained space of a tunnel aligned male contests so that they necessarily occurred as duels, and that final ingredient appears to have triggered an arms race.

Both branches and tunnels restrict the approach of an opponent, aligning fights so that they necessarily occur as duels. For many animals, like this Jackson's chameleon, battles over branches likely sparked the rapid evolution of their weapons.

Branches work the same way. In a sense, they are just "inside-out" tunnels, since a branch, like a tunnel, is linear and can be blocked.

This horned rodent (now extinct) appears to have fought over burrows.

Branches also align fights so that rivals have no choice but to approach one at a time, confronting opponents face-to-face (imagine a troll guarding a bridge). The beetles I first tried to study in Ecuador, *Golofa porteri*, fight over branches (bamboo shoots), as do many other types of rhinoceros beetle, as well as leaf-footed bugs with huge hind legs, stalk-eyed flies, and horned chameleons. In all of these species, a change in their behavior, fighting on branches, shifted their contests from scrambles to duels. And this simple change in behavior started an arms race.

Stalk-eyed flies fighting over a root must confront each other face-to-face in a duel.

There are even animals that fight out in the open that also fight in duels. In this case, however, it's the way the fights unfold that accomplishes the duel (rather than a branch or a tunnel). Males use their weapons to size each other up. Just like Homer's ancient heroes Achilles and Hector, they start with proud, side-by-side struts and waving displays. Then, if they are still matched, they'll poke and prod, sparring with the other male. If that doesn't work, pushes become jabs, and then stabs. The intensity of these fights ratchets up in stages, escalating all the way only when opponents are very evenly matched.

Even fights that happen out in the open can turn out to be duels, if the rivals assess each other beforehand, and only escalate to dangerous battle in stages.

Fights like this don't happen by accident, or by surprise. They escalate slowly and predictably, and by the time they get dangerous they are always one-on-one. Deer and elk fight this way, as do caribou and ibex. Even out in the open, their fights fulfill our essential prerequisite of unfolding as duels.

CHAPTER 20

Billboards of Battle

Once I'd started comparing animal and military weapons, I couldn't stop. I realized as I pored through accounts of tanks and battleships, airplanes and nuclear weapons, that all of these stories were the same. The parallels between animal and military weapons were incredible. Not only did both sorts of arms race *start* for the same reasons (duels), but they also unfolded in the same ways too. In every instance, the arms race progressed through the exact same sequence of stages. One of these stages was deterrence.

Stages of an Arms Race:

1. Competition & duels trigger a race

2. Weapons get BIG

3. Weapons get expensive

4. Weapons become signals (Deterrence)

5. Cheaters invade

6. Arms race collapses (Weapons disappear)

7. Repeat . . .

As animal weapons begin to get big, they start functioning as signals in addition to actual battle. Only the best-conditioned males—the absolute top of the lot, with the best health, the largest body sizes, and the most stored energy reserves—only the best of the best can produce the really, really big weapons. Small males, or males in poor condition or health, simply cannot afford to pay the price. Their weapons are pathetic beside those of the very best males (simple spikes instead of the resplendent racks of the biggest bucks, for example). This means that *weapon size* becomes a pretty good indicator—a billboard—of the fighting ability of each male.

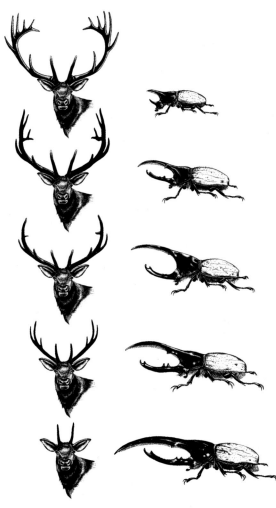

Big weapons are expensive, and only the best-conditioned males can afford to produce full-sized antlers or horns. Because of this, weapon size makes a perfect signal—a biological "billboard"—of the fighting ability of each male. Rivals start to use weapon size to decide whether to escalate a fight. In other words, big weapons make effective *deterrents*, dissuading smaller males from even attempting an outright battle.

Rivals start using weapon size to decide whether or not to escalate a fight. They don't just lunge into battle. They assess each other beforehand: Whose weapon is bigger? Because a male with bigger weapons really is likely to win, it often makes sense for smaller males to simply walk away.

Weapons start to act as signals—deterrents—settling contests without dangerous battle. Deterrence means that simply having a big weapon is enough to prevent rivals from attacking. In fact, in species with the biggest weapons of all, animals like caribou and fiddler crabs, the overwhelming majority of contests get settled this way. In one study of caribou, for example, thirteen thousand male contests were observed and only six escalated all the way to full battle. Six out of thirteen thousand! Caribou have the largest weapons relative to their body size of any living mammal, and almost all of their contests get settled *without a fight*.

Fallow deer sizing each other up. Weapons this big function as deterrents—signals of fighting ability that can settle contests simply by being big. Most of the time, the smaller male will walk away, opting not to enter into a dangerous brawl he almost certainly wouldn't win.

Fiddler crabs also use their weapons as deterrents, sizing up opponents in the early stages of battle. The smaller male usually backs down before the fight gets dangerous.

Deterrence leads to a surprising paradox: Across animals, the species with the biggest weapons are often the most peaceful. The males with the biggest weapons hardly ever have to use them in an actual fight. They certainly *can* fight, and if provoked they definitely will. But knock-down, drag-out battles tend to be surprisingly rare, and the net effect is peace.

We use our biggest military weapons as deterrents too. During the height of the British Empire, for example, "first-rate" sailing galleons were the world's most technologically advanced weapons. They were so powerful, in fact, that simply sailing one of these ships into troubled waters could settle political disputes on the spot. But building a ship like this cost a fortune. Most nations at that time couldn't afford to have any of these warships at all, yet Britain kept dozens and dozens in her fleet. This period, incidentally, was called the "Pax Britannica," or "British *Peace.*"

The United States uses its most expensive ships in the same way today. A *Nimitz*-class aircraft carrier and its associated strike group

During the height of the British Empire, sailing "ships of the line" made superb deterrents. Simply sailing one of these ships into troubled waters was often enough to settle a conflict.

The United States uses her aircraft carriers in the same way today. Carrier strike groups function as deterrents more often than as weapons of battle.

costs more than $20 billion (the brand-new Gerald Ford–class carriers cost even more). The United States has eleven of these carrier strike groups; no other nation has even one. Massive, powerful, and prohibitively expensive, our carriers function both as weapons and deterrents, portable projections of military power shuttled like chess pieces to stabilize troubled regions and implement our foreign policy.

I was convinced beyond a doubt now that caribou antlers and aircraft carriers worked the same way. Both had been swept into an arms race; both had attained huge sizes with staggering production costs; and both now worked as deterrents to settle confrontations without dangerous battle.

CHAPTER 21

Mutually Assured Destruction

The most impressive—and the scariest—arms race of all time was the Cold War, a military standoff between the Union of Soviet Socialist Republics (USSR) and her allies (called the "Warsaw Pact") on the one hand, and the United States and her allies (called "NATO") on the other. By the end of the Second World War, weapons technologies had taken a major leap with the invention of the first true weapons of mass destruction, nuclear bombs, which the United States dropped over Hiroshima and Nagasaki, Japan, in 1945. These weapons were so incredibly destructive that they horrified the world. They were "game changers" capable of deciding the outcome of a war outright. Nobody wanted to be caught without them. But they were also very difficult to manufacture and extraordinarily expensive. Only the wealthiest of nations could afford them, and, with most countries still reeling from the damage of the world war, that meant the United States and the USSR.

Both nations raced to develop as many nuclear weapons as they could. The Cold War shares many features with other arms races, including those of animals. For one thing, it was triggered by a duel—a showdown between two rival superpowers, the US and the USSR. This duel sparked a rush to develop bigger and bigger military forces, armed with better and better weapons. Submarines, fighter jets, aircraft carriers, bombers, missiles, and even the bombs themselves all got swept up in this race, as each superpower surged forward in an attempt to surpass the capabilities of its rival. From 1947 until 1991, the US and USSR raced to stay ahead of each other militarily, and the sizes of their military forces exploded.

Just as in animals, these weapons began to work as deterrents. Everybody feared what would happen if the superpowers entered into an unrestricted nuclear war, and fear of these consequences helped keep either side from attacking the other outright (this was called "mutually assured destruction," or MAD). Just like the antlers of caribou or the claws of fiddler crabs, simply having the biggest and best weapons was enough to prevent an outright unrestricted war. This period is called the "Cold War" precisely because neither side

Titan II missiles were nuclear weapons that functioned as deterrents during the Cold War.

ever did launch its nuclear weapons against the other (that, presumably, would have been a "Hot War").

Although the Cold War ended more than twenty-five years ago, the deadliest of these "Cold War" weapons remain with us. And they definitely still act as deterrents—even more effective deterrents than aircraft carriers and strike groups.

Modern nuclear warheads are thousands of times deadlier than the original bombs dropped over Hiroshima and Nagasaki, and collectively there are many thousands more of them in existence. Put bluntly, present-day nuclear weapons—were they actually to be used—could more than destroy all living people and most of everything else on the planet. And they could do this many hundreds of times over. These really are weapons designed to be *deterrents*, and we all have to hope that they never, ever get used.

The most effective (and expensive) nuclear weapons comprise a triad. Submarines lurk silently beneath the seas, always moving, difficult to track, and packed with missiles capable of delivering nuclear warheads to targets thousands of miles away. Bomber aircraft, launched in times of crisis and refueled as needed from midair, provide the second leg of the triad. Like submarines, these "stealth" bombers are difficult to locate, always moving and invisible. And they carry nuclear missiles too. Finally, land-based "intercontinental" missiles make up the third leg of the triad. The US has three bases with land-based intercontinental nuclear missiles (called Minuteman III missiles): one in Wyoming, one in North Dakota, and one in Montana not all that far from me.

Nuclear triads are designed to keep the missiles so spread out and hard to find that it would be impossible for any enemy to completely destroy all of them in a single strike. And, an effective triad is packed with enough missiles so as to be redundant; if some of the missiles *do* get taken out by an enemy, enough will still be left

Nuclear "triads" consist of land-based strategic missiles, nuclear submarines, and long-range stealth bombers such as this Stratofortress.

intact to destroy that enemy anyway. Welcome to the deadly logic of nuclear deterrence!

The technology required to maintain a nuclear triad is impressive, and the cost staggering—especially when you consider that it's not just the missiles, or the nuclear warheads on top of the missiles, but all the ships, planes, and underground silos, as well as the satellites and navigation systems, the sensor "nets" deployed to detect incoming missiles, and the high-tech command-and-control infrastructure. The US will have to spend more than one trillion dollars (a thousand billion) to keep its nuclear triad. In fact, modern nuclear triads are so incredibly expensive that only 2 percent of the world's nations can afford them: the United States, Russia, China, and India. That's about the same as the percentage of caribou bulls able to afford the most extreme antlers.

PART 6

When Arms Races Collapse

JOURNAL ENTRY 3 *Witnessing the Weapons Firsthand*

I got to visit one of our nuclear missile bases recently, and it was both exciting and scary. An Air Force captain kindly showed us around (I was traveling with a film crew from the British Broadcasting Corporation, or BBC, working on a documentary comparing animal and military weapons). On the wall of his office was a wide map of Montana sprinkled with 150 tiny dots—each one an underground silo containing a missile. These silos are scattered across a vast and barren landscape of more than thirteen thousand square miles.

The silos, in turn, are connected by a web of more than a thousand miles of underground cables, feeding into fifteen different underground control bunkers. Each buried bunker is a self-contained control center run by a crew of two, and each has the capability to launch all of the missiles from all of the other control centers. Redundancy. Unless all fifteen of these bunkers were destroyed simultaneously, our missiles could still be launched. And taking out even one of these buried control centers would be tricky, since they are surrounded by solid rock and encased in radiation-shielded, shock-absorbent shells built to withstand all but a direct-impact nuclear detonation. Taking all of them out at once would not be easy.

We even got to visit the training module—an exact replica of one of the underground control bunkers used daily by the crews to practice and train. I knew it was just a training room. But it didn't matter. Just being in there was awe-inspiring, and chilling. This is where the crews practiced *launch sequences*. Where they worked through the steps needed to turn the keys—four keys, by the way. Two per person, and spaced far enough apart that both people are needed. More redundancy. These were the keys that could end our world. One launch—just one of these missiles—could begin a deadly cascade that would destroy everything we know: cities, farmland, fisheries, families. These weapons would torch the sky, leaving enough radioactive contamination to make both land and water toxic for centuries.

Kids growing up today don't remember the Cold War, or the fear of knowing that at any moment your world could end. To them it feels like a distant past. They didn't have to do practice drills in school, like I did, sitting under their desks when the alarm sounded (like that would work!). But I remember. I'll always remember. And it sure felt real to me right then, as I sat in one of the control seats, surrounded by switches and panels and the workings of a modern-day nuclear missile base.

This wasn't a museum, or a relic of the past. Crews had been training in this room when we arrived, and a crew was waiting to train in there when we left. Twenty-four hours a day, every day, these same crews rotate in shifts to make sure that underground control bunkers across Montana, Wyoming, and North Dakota are ready—alert and able to launch at a moment's notice. They're sitting in those bunkers right now.

Standing in front of a Minuteman missile, Malmstrom Air Force Base, Montana, in 2016.

CHAPTER 22

The Beginning
of the End

So you're stuck in an arms race. Weapons are surging forward, evolving to bigger and bigger sizes—more elaborate, more extravagant, and much more expensive. Sure, this makes them great deterrents, billboards honestly advertising the fighting ability of an opponent. They work as deterrents because only the richest nations or the biggest, healthiest bulls and bucks—only the wealthy—can afford to pay the extraordinary costs. And, let's be fair; they *work* if you happen to be that biggest buck or you live in the wealthiest nation.

What does everybody else do? Supposing you're *not* the biggest male in the herd? You're smaller and weaker—life didn't smile on you the way it did them. What do you do if you can't afford the biggest and best weapons? You cheat.

Cheating is rampant in the animal world. Once you start to look for it, you find it everywhere. Take dung beetles, for example. I'd discovered cheating years ago in my beetle farms on Barro Colorado Island. The biggest, best males have the horns. They win the fights, and they guard the entrances to tunnels containing females. Tiny males can't afford big horns, so they don't bother producing any horns at all. And these little guys definitely don't play by the rules. Instead of fighting a losing battle at the tunnel entrance, they dig their own tunnel—a side tunnel—that intersects the guarded tunnel beneath the guarding male. In this way they can slip into a tunnel undetected, and, when they do, they go straight to the female, mate, and leave, in and out of the tunnel in as little as ten minutes.

A sneaky male cuttlefish slips in between a courting male and his female.

Sneakers like this lurk in all sorts of animal populations. The smallest male cuttlefish (marine mollusks related to the octopus) cloak themselves in colors that look like females, sidling up next to a courting male and slipping in between that male and his female. Sneaky male salmon zip into a territory, raining down sperm in a cloud over a female's eggs, in and out again so fast that the territorial male can't stop him. Sneaky bighorn sheep do much the same thing. They race into a big ram's territory to mate with females while he's distracted in a fight.

A small male salmon (bottom center) sneaks into another male's territory, raining down sperm in a cloud over a female's eggs.

In species after species, males who can't play by the rules *break the rules* and cheat. Cheaters, I now realized, affect the whole dynamic of an arms race because they steal reproductive success from the big-weaponed males. Heavily armed males still pay the full price of building and using their weapons—the *cost* of the weapons stays the same—but now the benefits they glean from having weapons get

Sneaky male bighorn sheep chase after females while the guarding male is distracted in a fight.

smaller. They still grow horns, and fight to guard the tunnel, but some of the offspring from that tunnel are sired by another male.

As long as the sneaky males steal only a little bit, not much changes. The benefits of big weapons stay huge, and the arms race surges forward. But when cheaters start doing *too* well, they can collapse an arms race. Suddenly, it's not worth it anymore to produce big weapons. The delicate balance between benefits and costs starts to tip the other way. Males without big weapons start doing better than those with them, and big weapons quickly disappear.

Cheaters erode the success of our biggest military weapons too, and they've done so for thousands of years. Guerilla tactics (also called *asymmetric warfare*) are a lot like sneaky male beetles and fish. Guerillas never wear military uniforms, for one thing. Instead, they hide, blending in with ordinary people in much the same way that sneaky males look and act like females. This makes them much harder to spot as an enemy. They also strike with quick, sneaky lunges, not open one-on-one duels. And they use makeshift, inexpensive weapons, like Molotov cocktails, pipe bombs, and improvised explosive devices (IEDs).

Here too, as with animals, as long as the cheaters don't inflict too

Guerrilla, or terrorist, tactics are a lot like sneaky male beetles and fish. These tactics use only inexpensive (e.g., homemade) weapons like this IED, and the sneakers themselves "hide." They dress like civilians, rather than soldiers, and rush up to targets in quick dashes.

Weapons technologies that "cheat" can collapse an arms race, causing expensive weapons to suddenly become obsolete. For example, the English longbow and gunpowder muskets marked the end for medieval armor.

Exploding shells ended the arms race for sailing galleons.

much damage, not much changes. State-of-the-art weapons continue to be well worth the price, and most people in the wealthy nation stay safe. The problem is that when cheating tactics start doing too well, then they can collapse an arms race overnight.

English longbows and gunpowder muskets spelled the end for medieval armor. Once suits of armor could be pierced, then suddenly it wasn't such a great idea to march into battle astride a horse like a big, bulky, shining target (a "knight in shining armor"). Just like that, armor went from being a fantastic form of protection to an expensive, heavy, bulky liability. So too exploding shells shattered the arms race for sailing warships, and submarines caused steam-powered "ironclad" battleships to be obsolete. In every case, and there are dozens, new strategies that broke the rules of engagement caused our most expensive weapons technologies to suddenly be obsolete, hugely expensive, and no longer worth the price.

I am absolutely convinced now that animal and military weapons really are the same. They each change in size and shape over time—they evolve. They each are molded by predictable—understandable—forces of selection, and, under the right circumstances, such as duels, they each can get sucked into escalating cycles of rapid evolution, or arms races.

Once caught up in such a race, both animal and military weapons quickly become so outrageously expensive that only the wealthy can afford them, and at that point they also become effective deterrents. "Billboards of battle" applied to aircraft carriers and antlers, beetle horns and nuclear missiles.

And now it was clear to me that even the *ends* of these arms races were the same. Animal and military arms races collapsed for precisely the same reason: Cheaters eroded the benefits of big weapons, causing them to be overpriced and obsolete. It was exciting, realizing that sneaky beetles and submarines did the same thing—that they each broke the rules of engagement in the same way. But the scientist in me had to keep pushing, following the logic as far as it would lead. What were the sneaky beetles of our world today? Do our most sophisticated weapons—our nuclear triads, for example—face a threat from sneaks and cheats?

It turns out they do. The sneaky strategy threatening our most sophisticated modern weapons is "cyberhacking."

SNEAKY SUBMARINES

After the age of sailing warships came a new type of arms race, this time for steam-powered ships with iron hulls called "ironclads." These new battleships carried much bigger guns able to strike with accuracy targets several miles away. Battleships also made splendid deterrents, bristling with powerful artillery and protected by walls of armor. But from the beginning they were vulnerable to sneaky strikes from below. Small and silent, submarines could approach even the biggest battleships undetected, firing torpedoes without ever breaching the surface. Much as tiny dung beetles burrow into tunnels beneath the guarding males, submarines sunk battleships by shattering their hulls from below.

Because of the threat of submarines, battleships had to be escorted wherever they went, surrounded by fleets of smaller ships whose job was to detect and intercept submarines before they could get to the bigger, more expensive battleship. Today, our aircraft carriers travel with a surrounding screen of smaller ships, called the "strike group," for exactly the same reason.

Torpedoed battleship viewed through the periscope of a submarine.

CHAPTER 23

Sneaky Beetles and Cyberhackers

The United States has the most advanced weapons in the world. Brand-new Gerald Ford–class aircraft carriers are incredible, as are our F-35 Strike Fighters. These new technologies are so expensive—they each cost hundreds of billions of dollars to develop—that they function both as weapons and as deterrents. But all of our newest weapons share the same weakness. They're each vulnerable for the same reason. None of them work without computers and software.

Cyberhackers are just like sneaky male dung beetles, worming their way into our software systems surreptitiously and lurking undetected. The United States has actually been hacked several times already. In 2004 the Chinese military broke into a suite of our state-of-the-art weapons systems, in a cyber-event called "Titan Rain," and in 2013 we caught them at it again. The scariest part is they weren't simply stealing secrets. They were inserting code. Called "zero-day attacks," these scripts were designed to lurk undetected and, had they

F-35 Strike Fighter. Supersonic, stealth, and supermaneuverable, these incredible aircraft cost more than $400 billion to design and build.

not been discovered, they would have given the Chinese military complete control of our weapons systems. By activating these hidden programs, they might have turned our most expensive weapons against us.

Cyberhackers are behaving just like sneaky male beetles, cuttlefish, and bighorn sheep; the "cheaters" of our tech-savvy digital age. Unfortunately, this analogy brings with it a rather startling question: Might our most advanced weapons too soon be obsolete? Like medieval armor and battleships before them, simply no longer worth the price?

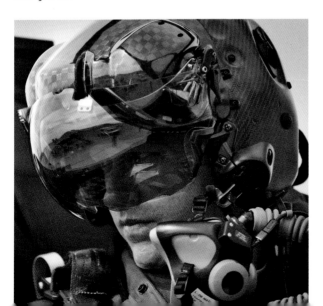

Each pilot's helmet costs more than half a million dollars. F-35 pilots have unobstructed views in all directions, including below the aircraft, thanks to seamless integration with arrays of cameras and sensors in the skin of the aircraft.

JOURNAL ENTRY 4 *Carrier Landing*

150 miles per hour to a full stop in two seconds. That's what happens when you land on an aircraft carrier. They'd warned us beforehand: it wouldn't be like anything we'd ever experienced. When commercial planes come in for a landing they slow down, almost to a stall. At the last second they pull the flaps down and flare nose up, touching down as gently as they can to provide a smooth ride for passengers.

You can't do that on an aircraft carrier. The deck is so short that pilots have to grab a cable with a "tailhook"—yanking the plane to an abrupt halt. And they don't slow down beforehand either, because if they miss the cable they need to be moving fast enough to careen right off the end of the deck for another try. So pilots come in fast and slam the plane down hard, scraping the tailhook along the metal deck toward the cable. Bang, screech, jerk, stop.

As passengers on a little Navy cargo plane called a C2 Greyhound, we had to experience all of this in the dark—there were no windows—and backwards, since the seats faced the wrong way. But it was worth it, because we stepped out of that plane into another world, getting a rare glimpse of fighter-aircraft operations out at sea.

After two years of waiting, I'd finally been selected. I was part of a tiny civilian ensemble flown out to the U.S.S. *Carl Vinson* (CVN-70) to witness carrier operations firsthand. We met the captain, the commanding officer, and the command master chief, as well as many of the crew. We stood on the flight deck as brand-new F-35 Strike Fighters slammed down before us—just 20 feet away—screaming past and jerking to a halt, before taxiing to a catapult and launching off the deck to try the whole thing again. This was one of the first times F-35s had ever landed on an aircraft carrier, and the pilots were all practicing the procedure over and over. That night we watched more landings from a balcony on the control tower, surrounded by the roar of engines and the sharp tang of jet fumes, all orchestrated to perfection in the darkness.

Now it was time to head back. I closed my eyes, grabbed the shoulder straps of my harness to make sure they were snug, and held my breath as our little plane hurtled off the flight deck, a steam-powered catapult flinging us into the sky. I had a lot to think about. I was incredibly impressed by what I'd seen. The technology was astounding, as was the professionalism and proficiency of the crew. Shuttling that many planes on such a small deck is no easy task. But to a person, they'd all agreed: successful operations depend critically on software. Landing the planes, steering the ship, navigating, communicating—even controlling the nuclear reactor that powers the ship—all of this requires sophisticated state-of-the-art programs. And that means all of it is potentially vulnerable to hackers.

The Navy knows this, of course, and has built-in fail-safes and layers of redundancies. And just as our enemies try to hack into our systems, so too our "cyber soldiers" are busy hacking into theirs. It's the newest twist on the arms race as nations wage a cyber war to control the weapons of their opponents. We're definitely not there yet, but the day may not be that far away when sneaky cyberhackers render even these extraordinary weapons obsolete.

Preparing for a "carrier landing."

We landed in the dark and backwards, jerking to a stop as the tailhook of our plane caught the cable.

F-35 fighters up close on the flight deck of the U.S.S. *Carl Vinson*. Steam gushes out of the tracks each time a catapult launches a plane.

TTI/Vanguard bills itself as an "advanced technology conference series" for senior-level corporate executives. Chief technical officers and chief financial officers from major corporations like Coca-Cola, ExxonMobil, Federal Express, Google, Nokia, Lockheed Martin, and Microsoft come together with senior personnel from the military and government to discuss tech-related issues and hash out ideas for the future.

This particular conference I was attending was devoted to cybersecurity—protecting information critical to both business and the safety of our country. In the past two days I'd met one of the men in charge of planning and purchasing new weapons for the

The "heads-up display" of a modern fighter pilot. Pilots can't fly modern fighters without software.

Department of Defense; I'd met the chief computer gurus (the people in charge of IT) at the Federal Bureau of Investigation, the Central Intelligence Agency (CIA), and the US Treasury; I'd even met the only man ever to serve as director of *both* the CIA and the National Security Agency—this is literally the guy who gave the president of the United States his daily security briefing!

Here were a hundred of the most brilliant people I'd ever seen, all gathered in a conference room at the Ritz-Carlton hotel for two days to present and listen to talks on the dangers of cyberterrorism, an emerging theater of war now considered to be "threat number one" to the safety of our country. Insidious and sneaky, hackers attempt to worm into our weapons systems all the time. The military has some impressive firewalls protecting our weapons. But every now and again someone manages to slip past the barriers undetected, working their way into our computer code and inserting little scripts

All of our most advanced weapons technologies depend critically on computers and software, which makes them vulnerable to a new kind of cheater: cyberhackers.

that hide there, dormant and waiting, ready to hijack our weapons and hand control over to the other side.

This was the problem we'd gathered in Washington, DC, to discuss. I was their keynote speaker—the last talk of the lot. These were the people tasked with addressing our nation's most imminent threat, the protectors of our military technology and government infrastructure. And I was going to talk to them about animal weapons.

Here was a new kind of fear for me—not the dread of being stranded in the steamy dark of a strange country, or being surrounded by lions in a flimsy tent. This was the fear of having to stand before a mighty audience and give a presentation they were not expecting, sharing with them a parallel they had never considered, and offering a bold idea: that we can learn from animal weapons. Just as I had learned from military scholars, so too the military might be able to learn from biology.

"Don't trip" was the first thought that flashed through my head as I stepped over the electric cables and headed up to the podium and into the lights. What was I doing here? I don't design firewalls, missiles, or battleships. I don't work for the CIA, and I definitely don't brief the president! I'm a *biologist*. I study beetles. Awesome beetles with amazing weapons, but beetles just the same. National security was a big leap from muddy boots in the rain forest. Could the secrets of beetle horns *really* help explain cyberhackers too?

TTI VANGUARD

Extreme Weapons

Doug Emlen
University of Montana

CYBERSECURITY

SEPTEMBER 27-28, 2016
WASHINGTON, D.C.

TTIVANGUARD.COM

Giving my talk at the TTI/Vanguard Cybersecurity Conference, in Washington, DC.

The answer of course was yes, and now I had to step up onto that stage and give my presentation, showing the industry leaders—the *builders* of battleships and designers of software—why they should care. Why we all should care.

CHAPTER 24

Full Circle

Maybe this wasn't such a good idea. I'd forgotten just how *hot* Panama was, and humid. Coming from Montana in November, where the mountain air was crisp and clear, the contrast could not have been more brutal. We pushed through the doors of the Panama City airport and stood there, gasping. Before we'd even finished walking through the parking lot our shirts were sticky with sweat, and by the time we made it out to the field station on Barro Colorado Island I was rethinking the whole trip.

I was here with my family, showing my children where I'd started my career as a biologist more than twenty years ago. I'd told them about tropical forests, about big leaves and monkeys, toucans, geckos, butterflies, and beetles. I'd even been silly enough to promise them a sloth, a gangly, shaggy creature that is almost impossible to spot because it hardly ever moves. Yet somehow I'd forgotten to warn them about the heat.

After unpacking in our cabin we dressed for the forest, pulling rubber boots over long, baggy slacks tucked into socks (to keep the ticks and chiggers out, of course); long sleeves; cotton bandannas; and wide-brimmed hats to divert any downpours from our eyes and face. Cory, fifteen, led the way, and not ten yards up the trail he stumbled face-first into a spiderweb. *Nephila*, shimmering three-inch-long spiders, had a habit of stretching their sticky strings across trails, and I'd forgotten to warn him to hold a stick in front of his face as he hiked. Fortunately, this spider wasn't as big as *Nephila* and I helped pull the tangle off his neck. Now Nicole, twelve, was being devoured by mosquitoes. Why they favor her I'll never know, but already a mini-swarm clustered around her exposed wrists, and her fingers were mottled red and puffy. I'd forgotten about mosquitoes too.

How is it that I'd neglected to think of these things? How could heat, spiders, and mosquitoes not be the *first* things I'd thought of when I relived my days in the forest? I guess because I'm a biologist. I love life in all of its varied forms, and no place pulses with the

Nephila spider on Barro Colorado Island.

Nicole and Cory, ready to explore the Panama forest.

vibrant profusion of life more spectacularly than a rain forest. For me, the irritation of humidity and chiggers paled beside the thrill of parrots, or the wonder of agoutis—awkward, rabbit-sized rodents gnawing stubbornly on rock-hard seeds underfoot—or monkeys! The deafening, throaty roar of a howler monkey, shaking branches and staring down, locking eyes with you from overhead—how could anyone not be thrilled by that?

But my children were *not* biologists—the realization now dawned on me as we stood there sweating in the pest-infested mud. Their passions lay elsewhere, with music and math and art—not monkeys or parrots, and certainly not beetles. I began to appreciate for the first time that for them, on this, their first-ever steps into a rain forest, the tropics appeared an overwhelming tangle of green, of vines and thorns and sticky mud, cloaked in a heat so oppressive it was staggering. This sacred return to my old stomping grounds might just be a colossal family mistake.

To their credit they marched on, tromping deeper into the dark understory, and, ever so slowly, the thrill began to ignite. A motmot—a stunning bird of blue and orange, paddle-like tail swishing back and forth—landed on a perch right in front of us, pulling our minds away from the mosquitoes. Then a toucan squawked past the trees overhead, green-and-yellow bill like an oversized banana pushed in front of its face. The more we saw the more fun the forest became, and by the time we found our first monkeys the exhilaration was complete.

My daughter was the first to notice the beetles, brown and yellow scarabs pushing pea-sized balls of dung. While the rest of us gaped up at the monkeys, she'd looked down, at the rotting leaves beneath our feet. The moment she showed me the beetles all my memories came flooding back: the sounds, the eerie feel of the forest, even the smells—the musky odors of monkeys, mold, mud, and, of course, the sweet, pungent scent of howler monkey dung (howler monkeys ferment leaves in their gut, so their dung does not smell at all like what we normally think of).

In they came, hovering inches over the leaf litter, tumbling down beside pieces of howler monkey dung. Squat and awkward, like tiny tortoises, little brown beetles plowed into the dung, pushing through it to the burrows below. With a twig we flipped over the bit of dung, revealing entrances to four little tunnels. No larger than the eraser on a new pencil, a male with two horns sprouting from his head waddled over to an opening and plunged in. These were the beasts I'd spent thousands of hours watching. Their battles had lured me to the tropics; their weapons motivated my career.

I was back.

I'd promised my kids rain, thundering downpours like they'd never seen before. Water slamming down in sheets so hard the ground shook and you had to scream to be heard over the pounding on the metal roof. It never happened. All week we looked to the sky, hot and sticky from dirt and sweat, hoping for a deluge. All we got was drizzle.

There they were, twenty years later. Ball-rolling beetles on the forest floor.

We'd tried to find my secret waterfall, and failed at that as well. For some reason "Nemesia" trail hadn't been maintained, and twenty years' tangle made the route impassable. But the birds cooperated. Shining flashes of blue and green—tanagers darting through the bushes—and parrots gliding overhead two by two on their way to a communal roost. We got to watch toucans and motmots, and two types of trogon—all of my favorites. The monkeys cooperated too. We saw lots of troops of howlers, and even found a rare family of Geoffroy's tamarins.

My original dorm room was long gone, the building torn down years ago, and my lab was gone too. Almost nothing remained of the rickety buildings of the "old lab"—that cluster perched two hundred steps up, high on the crest of the hill. But one of the buildings still stood, the old dining hall, perched high above the harbor. Renovated and turned into a museum of sorts, it now had a broad balcony on the second floor that offered sweeping views over the treetops, all the way out to the lake and canal below. Boats chugged by, way out in the channel, crisscrossing north and south between oceans. From here they looked like little ants.

Looking for beetles.

What an incredible feeling to be back, feet perched on this beautiful balcony, so close to where it all started, and to share this magical place with my family. It's amazing, really, when I think about it. I'd learned so much here, about biology—about life. Who'd have thought that little beetles studded with tiny horns could reveal so much? *Dung* beetles, even. That the battles they fought held clues to the mystery of weapons everywhere—in crabs or caribou, elephants, elk, and humans? And how incredible that insights from these same little beetles might help us understand our own weapons, the political realities we grapple with in our everyday lives—even threats to our national security! That's why I love science. You just never know where the questions will take you.

What will Cory's and Nicole's questions be? What will *yours* be?

Nicole's drawing of a motmot.

Epilogue

Science is always a journey. It's a journey for the mind, as we painstakingly assemble clues, conduct experiments, and arrange the pieces of our intellectual puzzle to answer a question. Answering the question usually just leads to another question. And another. But that's okay, because this is how the process of science works. Science is all about discovering. It's the way we gently unravel the mysteries of life, figuring out things that nobody has ever figured out before.

Sometimes science is also a journey in the literal sense too, since the quest for answers can pull us into the strangest of places. My journey definitely involved wild places like South America, the rain forests of Central America, volcanic swamps of Australia, and African savannas. It even took me to our nation's capital to meet with leaders of the military, FBI, and CIA—*that* was an unexpected twist! And it took me to Montana, the beautiful place I now call home.

It's now 2019, twenty-nine years since I began my beetle studies in Ecuador. I still conduct research on beetles, and I still teach my classes at the University of Montana. But I've also spent the past few years immersed in military literature, going back and forth between animal and military weapons and sharing the parallels with as many people as I can. I began by giving talks at biology departments in universities around the country, and soon started giving talks to broader audiences too, like outreach presentations at natural history museums and high schools. I've recorded interviews for National Public Radio and YouTube. I even got to work with a film crew from the British Broadcasting Corporation (BBC) on a documentary on these ideas for the BBC and NOVA.

Still, the parallels stun me. Seriously, who'd have ever thought that beetles could teach us anything useful about battleships, or about national security? That's a long way from where my journey started. But that's the thrill—the *adventure*—of science: You never know where the questions will take you.

Acknowledgments

This is my first attempt at crafting a book for young adult readers, and I have many people to thank. This book would not be what it is had it not been for the guidance and persistence of my editor at Roaring Brook, Emily Feinberg. She was brilliant in her suggestions and had no qualms about sending me "back to the drawing board" as many times as it took to get it right. I love what this book finally became, and I owe much of that to her. I also benefited greatly from the guidance of Dorothy Hinshaw Patent, who took time away from her own writing on multiple occasions to help me through this process. Monique Sterling provided beautiful illustrations for this book and skillfully designed it. Tess Weitzner helped with logistics and photo permissions. Melinda Ackell and Kerry Johnson expertly copyedited and proofread the text many times. David Tuss provided illustrations for *Animal Weapons*, many of which are reprinted here. My literary agent, Tina Bennett, and her talented assistant, Svetlana Katz, were helpful throughout the process and continue to support me. Early versions of this manuscript benefited from the suggestions of a number of colleagues and family members, including especially Alexis Billings, Kerry Bright-Emlen, Natalia Demong-Emlen, Nicole Emlen, Alison Perkins, Sarah Solie, and Kelly Webster. I'd like to thank the editor of my book *Animal Weapons: The Evolution of Battle* (Henry Holt, 2014), Gillian Blake, for first having the idea that I write a young adult narrative nonfiction book to accompany *Animal Weapons*, and for helping to make it happen. I thank the National Science Foundation for continuing to fund my research program. And I thank my wife, Kerry, and my children, Cory and Nicole, for always being there for me and for making my life such a wonderful adventure.

Resources

This book is a spinoff of sorts—the "story behind the story"—for the book *Animal Weapons: The Evolution of Battle* (Henry Holt, 2014). Readers interested in greater depth of coverage of the biological ideas discussed in this book should turn to *Animal Weapons,* and full citations of the extensive primary literature are provided in that volume.

However, for a few topics in particular, I would like to recommend the following books.

For readers interested in the early writings of the French naturalist Jean-Henri Fabre, many of his works have been translated into English and are surprisingly readable. My favorite is *Fabre's Book of Insects* (Dover, 2013), a retelling of Fabre's book *Souvenirs Entomologiques* (1891) based on the translation by Alexander Teixeira de Mattos. This is a gorgeously illustrated series of vignettes about the remarkable lives of insects. I also highly recommend *The Insect World of J. Henri Fabre* by Alexander Teixeira de Mattos (reprinted by Beacon Press, 1991). Finally, if you can find it, I recommend *The Sacred Beetle and Others* (Jean-Henri Fabre, reprinted by The Minerva Group, 2002).

If you are interested in learning more about the amazing natural history of dung beetles, I suggest starting with *The Nesting Behavior of Dung Beetles (Scarabaeinae): An Ecological and Evolutive Approach* by Gonzalo Halffter (Instituto de Ecologia Mexico, 1982) and *The Natural History of Dung Beetles of the Subfamily Scarabaeinae* by Gonzalo Halffter and Eric G. Matthews (Medical Books, 1999). Finally, although it's a bit more technical, I recommend *Ecology and Evolution of Dung Beetles,* a compilation of works by leading authors edited by Leigh W. Simmons and T. James Risdill Smith (Wiley-Blackwell, 2013).

For more general treatments of sexual selection the classic is of course *The Descent of Man, and Selection in Relation to Sex* by Charles Darwin (1871; reprinted by Freeman, 1977). More recent treatments of this topic include *Sexual Selection* by Malte Andersson (Princeton, 1992) and the less technical *Sexual Selection* (Scientific American Library) by James L. Gould and Carol Grant Gould (W. Freeman & Co., 1989). Finally, it focuses on insect examples, but a current and in-depth treatment of these ideas is provided in the volume edited by Leigh Simmons and David Shuker, *The Evolution of Insect Mating Systems* (Oxford, 2014).

For books examining the evolution of military technologies, I highly recommend *Soul of the Sword: An Illustrated History of Weaponry and Warfare from Prehistory to the Present* by Robert O'Connell and illustrated by John Batchelor (Free Press, 2002). This is highly readable and intuitive, but if you want greater depth of coverage, then definitely read Robert O'Connell's *Of Arms and Men: A History of War, Weapons, and Aggression* (Oxford, 1990). I also recommend *The Evolution of Weapons and Warfare* by Colonel Trevor N. Dupuy (Da Capo Press, 1990). Finally, if you'd like a vivid description of the soldier's perspective in ancient battles, I was impressed by *The Face of Battle: A Study of Agincourt, Waterloo, and the Somme* by John Keegan (Penguin, 1983).

Photo Credits

Page 1: Monique Sterling; 10 (top): Carl Buell; 12: Geoff Galice / Wikimedia Commons; 13: Wayne Hsu; 29 (top): Smithsonian Tropical Research Institute; 38: Monique Sterling; 41: David Tuss; 43: Monique Sterling; 44: Monique Sterling; 49: Monique Sterling; 55: Monique Sterling; 56: Monique Sterling; 66: Patricia Backwell; 67 (top): Ryan Hagerty / Wikimedia Commons; 67 (bottom): Shutterstock; 69: Monique Sterling; 76–77: Stephen T. Emlen / Natalie Demong; 80 (top): Monique Sterling; 80 (bottom): Casey Allen / Pixabay; 81: Cheryl Ramalho / Shutterstock; 83 (top): Denali National Park / Wikimedia Commons; 83 (bottom): Wikimedia Commons; 84 (top): Pixabay; 84 (bottom): Shutterstock; 85: Robert Niese; 86: NewellConverse Wyeth (1882–1945) / Wikimedia Commons; 88 (left): su neko / Wikimedia Commons; 88 (right): Gailhampshire / Wikimedia Commons; 89: Alfred Yan; 91 (top): Monique Sterling; 91 (bottom): Udo Schmidt / Wikimedia Commons; 94–95: Pixabay; 99 (top): Heidi Trudell / Big Bend Nature; 99 (bottom): Don Christian; 100: Rado Javor; 104 (top): Louis-Philippe Crépin (1772–1851) / Wikimedia Commons; 104 (bottom): Jean d'Wavrin; 106: Jean d'Wavrin, *The Battle of Aljubarrota* / British Library / Wikimedia Commons; 107 (top): Wildfire Games; 107 (bottom): Domenick D'Andrea, *The Delaware Regiment at the Battle of Long Island* / US Federal Government / Wikimedia Commons; 108: German Army / Wikimedia Commons; 109: Peter Paul Rubens (1577–1640) *Achilles Slays Hector* / Wikimedia Commons; 115: Rado Javor; 116: "HMS Agamemnon and Commodore Nelson's squadron, Mediterranean 1796, by Geoff Hunt PPRSMA"; 117: Mark Miller; 118: Paulus Hector Mair Tjost / Wikimedia Commons; 121: Shutterstock; 122 (top): R. Bruce Horsfall / Wikimedia Commons; 122 (bottom): Sam Cotton; 123: Johan Swanepeoel / Shutterstock; 124: Monique Sterling; 125: David Tuss; 126: Alamy; 127: Patricia Backwell; 128 (top): "Randolph against the odds, 7th March 1778, by Geoff Hunt PPRSMA"; 128 (bottom): Aspersions / Wikimedia Commons; 131: US Air Force / Airman 1st Class Justin Armstrong / 5th Bomb Wing Public Affairs / Wikimedia Commons; 133: Stuart Dunn; 139: Roger Hanlon; 140: Johnny Armstrong / USGS; 141: David Swindler; 142 (top): United States Department of Defense / Wikimedia Commons; 142 (bottom): Andrew Spratt; 143: Thomas Luny (1759–1837) / Wikimedia Commons; 145: National Archives and Records Administration / Wikimedia Commons; 147 (top): Staff Sgt. Jensen Stidham / US Air Force / Wikimedia Commons; 147 (bottom): SrA Brett Clashman / Wikimedia Commons; 150 (bottom): US Navy; 151: Telstar Logistics / Wikimedia Commons; 152: US Navy; 153: TTI / Vanguard

The following images are courtesy of the author:
Page 2, 3, 9, 10 (bottom), 11, 15, 16, 17, 20, 21, 23, 24, 25, 29 (bottom), 30, 31, 32, 33, 37, 39, 40, 46, 59, 60, 61, 63, 65, 92, 93, 97, 98, 137, 149, 150 (top), 155, 156, 158, 159, 160

Index